TRIUMPHS
of the
HEART

Crossway books by Cheryl Ford

The Pilgrim's Progress Devotional
Treasures from the Heart: The Value of Godly Character
Healing for the Heart: The Hope of Full Surrender
Triumphs of the Heart: The Promise of Joyful Living

WOMEN OF THE WORD

TRIUMPHS
of the
HEART

*The Promise of
Joyful Living*

CHERYL FORD

CROSSWAY BOOKS

A DIVISION OF
GOOD NEWS PUBLISHERS
WHEATON, ILLINOIS

Library of Congress Cataloging-in-Publication Data
Ford, Cheryl
    Triumphs of the heart : the promise of joyful living / Cheryl Ford.
        p.   cm.— (Women of the Word)
    Includes bibliographical references.
    ISBN 1-58134-369-8 (alk. paper)
    1. Women in the Bible—Biography. 2. Christian women—Religious life.
I. Title. II. Series: Ford, Cheryl, Women of the Word.
BS575 .F673   2002
220.9'2'082—dc21   2001006186
                                                                        CIP

15	14	13	12	11	10	09	08	07	06	05	04	03	02
15	14	13	12	11	10	9	8	7	6	5	4	3	2	1

Dedicated to the victims
of the world's worst act of terrorism
and to their families.

Out of the ashes of devastation
may God bring hope, restoration, and triumph.

Contents

ACKNOWLEDGMENTS   9

PREFACE   11

1. ANNA: The Watchful Heart   13

2. THE SYROPHOENICIAN WOMAN: 37
   The Tenacious Heart

3. THE QUEEN OF SHEBA: The Searching Heart   59

4. DEBORAH: The Valiant Heart   79

5. QUEEN ESTHER: The Daring Heart   107

6. PRISCILLA: The Liberated Heart   139

7. THE WOMAN WITH TWO MITES: 169
   The Sacrificial Heart

8. THE WOMAN AT THE WELL: 195
   The Good-News Heart

NOTES   223

ACKNOWLEDGMENTS

Thanks again to my husband, Clay, who prays for me, encourages me, and tells me to get back to work. I would not be doing this without his gracious support.

Thanks so much to Jean Abercrombie and the rest of my incredible AFBC church family. Many of them prayed for me faithfully, and I didn't even know it. They have been patient and loving as my writing took me away from many church activities.

Thanks to my E-mail buddies for their prayers: Jean Bailes, Lory Chaves, Marie Dainow, Kathleen DeVita, Gail Gordon, Helen Mooradkanian, Sharon Schlotzhauer, Pat Schmitz, Kersti Stoen, Linda Storm, Terry Temple, Jean Wilson. I am so grateful also for the encouragement and prayers of my wonderful mother-in-law, Virginia Ford, and the best daughter a mother could have, my daughter Hannah. I want to thank my sister Gayle Anderson for helping to research the various biblical women. My thanks go also to my son and daughter-in-law, Billy and Denise, for their love, understanding, and support.

I praise the Lord for Marvin Padgett, Jill Carter, and others at Crossway Books who so faithfully carry out their ministries for God's glory. I am especially thankful to my editor and friend, Lila Bishop, for her wisdom and expertise. As always it's a joy to entrust a manuscript to her capable hands.

But the praise and glory belong to Jesus Christ, our wondrous Savior and Lord. He has taken our sin-blackened hearts, cleansed us and given us new life. Now the very wind of heaven blows through us, lifting our hearts in joy and triumph. Thank You, Lord!

PREFACE

Recently I turned on the evening news to hear nothing but bad news. Toward the end of the broadcast, the newsman said, "Finally, some good news—the stock market went up today." Good news? Well, only till the next trading session when it took another nosedive.

If only the world would look for good news in the right place. God's people have heard and received exceedingly good news. Throughout history they have tuned in to God and stood on His wondrous promises. Claiming His resources of wisdom, strength, and stability, even in the darkest and most tumultuous hours, they have risen in faith and courage to experience great triumphs.

While God is no respecter of persons, He is forever a respecter of hearts. What types of hearts find blessing and triumph? What kind come through their ordeals with "shouts of joy" (Psalm 105:43)? In this book, we will return to the Bible to meet some of God's women. Unable to see them face to face, we will get to know them heart to heart. They were real women with real hopes and dreams, who lived through real stress and some even through deep trauma.

They didn't all know it, but these were women whom God prepared for greatness, women of purpose and victory in times of destiny. Receiving a vision from God for their lives, they rose to triumph over the fears, adversity, and even complacency that could defeat them. Blazing new trails, refusing to take no for an answer, they shook nations and changed history. How their stories should encourage us! If these women could live triumphantly for God, then why can't God use us, too?

This is no time for hunkering down and withdrawing from the fray. Though we live in a dark and dangerous time, it is also a challenging, incredible, and marvelous time of destiny for the church.

Filled with unparalleled opportunities for advancing God's kingdom, this is a time for the women of God to rise up with fresh purpose and dedication. In this book, we, like the women we consider, will learn to seek and know the Lord better and to become strong, bold, and victorious to His glory.

The Lord calls to us, "Women of God, arise! I have joyous triumphs for you!" Let's respond to His call. Let's open our hearts and hear His truth. Let's receive His marching orders, go into the Promised Land, and lay claim to our spiritual inheritance. Let's blaze new trails and spread the good news boldly to our generation.

Have you heard the call? My prayer is that you will hear it ringing loudly and clearly through these pages. Despite all the bad news around us, God is doing marvelous things today! God's slumbering church is rising in faith to meet the challenges before us. We are rediscovering spiritual resources for victory available to us in Christ. We are engaging our enemy, the devil, and he is losing ground. Christ will return soon for His triumphant and glorious bride, and He wants *you* included in the ranks. This is your time of destiny!

Shouts of joy and victory resound in the tents of the righteous: "The LORD's *right hand has done mighty things!"*

PSALM 118:15

But thanks be to God, who always leads us in triumphal procession in Christ and through us spreads everywhere the fragrance of the knowledge of him.

2 CORINTHIANS 2:14

1

THE WATCHFUL HEART

LUKE 2:36-38

PERHAPS THIS IS THE DAY! It was early morning, and the white-haired, elderly woman had barely finished rubbing her eyes before she was up and about. She looked old and decrepit, but looks can be deceiving. True, her body was bent and frail, but her enthusiasm was great and her fine-tuned senses sharp. Drawing a deep breath, she perused the temple's Court of Women as she had countless times before. *God is up to something,* she thought. *I know it. Very shortly He will bring Israel's redemption. It really might be today.* Just the thought was enough to brighten her eyes, quicken her heart, and liven her bones. *Oh, Lord, let it be today; let it be today!*

Anna loved the temple. It was her life. She felt so happy on those sacred grounds. In the early years she used to get up with the dawn, proceed up the temple mount, walk past the outer wall, through the portico, into the Court of the Gentiles, through the Beautiful Gate, and into the Court of Women. She tired of that though. One day she simply refused to leave. Subsequently, for more years than she could now recall, she had literally lived there. Old Anna the prophetess was always there praying and ministering to the Lord.

People began to straggle in. Most thought it would be just another day in the temple courts—business as usual. But, oh, how wrong they were! This day, anything but typical, would outshine them all. It fact, this day would be one for the books. Temple archives would have no record of a similar visitation. Even so, the momentous occurrence would slip on by for the most part unnoticed.

None of it, however, would escape Anna. Not only was she a temple fixture, but she walked with God, worshiping and praying constantly. He shared with her His truth, and through His enlightening presence, nothing significant related to Israel's spiritual life escaped her. And He had a splendid revelation in store for her that day. Yes, that very day her very long and faithful vigil would be rewarded.

Those proceeding into the temple grounds could always find Anna there—if they looked for her. But normally an elderly woman would attract little attention against the marvelous structure of cream stone and gold, the impressive colonnades, the pomp of the priests, and the heraldry of the guards. The majestic structure, still under construction by King Herod to impress the Jews, was quite enough to keep infrequent visitors absorbed in proud wonder.

Then there were others who frequented the temple—the priests, the guards, the moneychangers, and many more besides who regularly conducted affairs there. They could easily have known Anna. She was, after all, a prophetess. Even so, amid the hubbub of the busy courts, they probably gave her scant notice. These people occupied themselves with business—buying and selling, giving and taking offerings, enforcing and fulfilling legal requirements—you know, "God's business."

The "important" stuff kept them all preoccupied. Anna, however, had her own preoccupation—God Himself. She attended the many public expressions of worship—the morning and evening temple services and hours of prayer—but they were not nearly enough for her. So "she never left the temple but worshiped night and day, fasting and praying" (Luke 2:37). Having effectively cut herself off from every other human enterprise, she made God her sole pursuit. Her wholly consecrated life, ever bent toward knowing Him and His purposes, had become a perpetual fragrant offering.

It was a dark period of history for the Jewish people. The Roman Empire dominated the entire Mediterranean world, having conquered more territory than either the Greeks, Persians, or Egyptians. Not only did Caesar hold the Jewish territories firmly in his grip, but the Jewish nation had not been independent since Judah had fallen to the Babylonians nearly six hundred years before. Numerous foreign kings had come and gone. The Jews felt restless and impatient. Where was the Jewish king who had been promised so long ago?

Hundreds of years had passed since God had lifted the spirit of prophecy from the Jewish nation. Silent, He had literally kept His people waiting for eons. For them it was a confusing time. Some, remembering a history strewn with false hopes, had given up waiting for their Redeemer; others, ready to revolt for their freedom, favored forcing the hands of both God and Rome; still others had made the keeping of Jewish laws the heart of their religion. This was more than enough to occupy them.

Then there were those precious few, like Anna, who patiently hoped against hope. They steadfastly believed God's promises to His people—promises such as: "See, a king will reign in righteousness" (Isa. 32:1) and "Of the increase of his government and peace there will be no end" (Isa. 9:7). What distinguished Anna from most in this group, however, was that while they kept busy with living their lives—eating, drinking, working, playing, sleeping—she kept a constant watch. Ever looking for the Messiah's appearing, night and day she tirelessly prayed, fasted, watched, and waited. As she kept her faithful watch, she felt God stir her heart. He was reviving the long-dormant spirit of prophecy.

We can call Anna's heart a Watchful Heart. Fueled by her consuming belief in God's promise, she continually stoked the watchfire of her soul. Not only did she know that in the fullness of time the prophetic promises of a Redeemer would be satisfied, but she knew something else. "Surely," the Scriptures say, "the Sovereign LORD does nothing without revealing his plan to his servants the prophets" (Amos 3:7). Anna knew that something earthshakingly significant was about to burst upon the scene; the hour for which her people had so long waited was upon them. So she kept to her vigil—watching and praying, watching and praying, days dragging into years, and years into decades . . . and more decades.

Just how long had she spent in this manner? More years than she could remember. The Bible says that this daughter of Phanuel of the tribe of Asher had become a widow after only seven years of marriage. She had never remarried, thus becoming an unfortunate member of a disadvantaged class in Jewish society. Widowhood was often seen as a disgrace, and widows frequently lived in poverty and depended upon charity. In their vulnerability, they were often victims of exploitation.

But Anna had risen above her liabilities, choosing to use her condition for God's pleasure and purpose. No longer considering herself bereft, she lived a satisfied life of service to Him. Now she was of a "great age," a widow of some eighty-four years. If we can take this to be the number of years she had been widowed, she may have been by this time 105 years old. At the least, she was eighty-four. Whichever, this old woman was young in hope and spirit.

Possibly Anna lodged in the court in a place provided by temple charities for homeless people. Or perhaps since she was a prophetess, they had given her a place to stay where people might readily consult her regarding the truths of God. Then again she may have lived in a building next to the temple and come to the court early each morning to remain all day.

Whatever the exact case, Anna's heart testified with David, "One thing I ask of the LORD, this is what I seek: that I may dwell in the house of the LORD all the days of my life, to gaze upon the beauty of the LORD and to seek him in his temple" (Ps. 27:4). Oh, how she longed to behold His beauty in its fullness. So there she was, dwelling in God's house, seeking, inquiring, watching, waiting.

Don't think for a moment that Anna was some kind of a pious

recluse. She was not. She knew many people well—especially those who similarly looked forward to God's redemption. Keenly aware of what went on about her in the temple, she no doubt mingled with the people who came to worship and ministered prophetic words of encouragement to them.

On this particular day Anna may have already felt anticipation. Suddenly in the courtyard she noticed something unusual—loud sounds of joy and exultation. As she went to investigate, excitement rose in her. It was her friend Simeon! She regarded him highly. They had often discussed the coming Messiah, and he was as eager to lay eyes on Him as she was. Simeon was speaking with a young couple and seemed enthralled with the baby the woman cradled in her arms. Why, the old man had never looked this animated before!

Anna felt her blood pressure skyrocket. What was this tingling, this trembling, this churning, this—this strange emotional charge she felt? Little did she know that God was, at that very moment, sending His reply to her lifetime of faithful praying and preparing. The enduring object of her heart's passion was being presented before her very eyes.

Impulsively Anna moved in closer so she could hear. The nearer she got, the more she felt God's Spirit moving on her, igniting her soul with expectation. Her heart cried, *Oh, Lord, is this the One—the One we have been waiting for? Is this the blessed Redeemer?* By now her heart pounded wildly as the prophetic voice within her shouted, *"Yes! Yes! Yes!"*

Anna got to the spot just in time to see Simeon scoop the baby up in his arms and pray. "Sovereign Lord," he said with trembling voice, "as you have promised, you now dismiss your servant in peace. For my eyes have seen your salvation, which you have prepared in the sight of all people, a light for revelation to the Gentiles and for glory to your people Israel" (Luke 2:29-32).

Anna gasped; her knees nearly gave out. Then she watched as Simeon set his gaze on the young mother and began prophesying,

"This child is destined to cause the falling and rising of many in Israel, and to be a sign that will be spoken against, so that the thoughts of many hearts will be revealed." Then he solemnly added, "And a sword will pierce your own soul too" (Luke 2:34-35). Though Anna was herself a prophetess, the meaning of these words may have escaped her. Never mind. She knew all she needed to know. At long last, the Redeemer—her Redeemer and the hope of Israel—was here!

"The thoughts of many hearts will be revealed." Simeon's prophecy immediately began its fulfillment with Anna, and what did the revelation expose in her? A heart exploding with praise and exultation. After hearing Simeon's sobering prediction of a painful sword, Mary and Joseph must have been greatly encouraged by Anna's response. Wide-eyed with excitement, she ran to find everyone she knew who likewise looked forward to the Messiah's appearing. Joyfully confirming Simeon's words of prophecy, she told them, "He is here! Hallelujah! The Christ is here! I have seen Him with my own eyes!"

Jesus Christ would visit the temple many times during His lifetime. At twelve years of age His parents would find Him there among the teachers. Later Satan would tempt Him from its pinnacle. Within its courts, He would teach, heal, challenge hypocrisy, drive out moneychangers, and even receive glad hosannas from children (Matt. 4:5; 21:12, 14-15, 23; 23:16; Luke 19:45; 21:38). But here He was, the month-old Christ child on His very first temple visit—and Anna witnessed it.

Casual observers might have seen an ordinary-looking old woman on a seemingly ordinary Jerusalem day. But through her expectant watching and praying, she had helped prepare the way for her Messiah's advent. Consequently, God gave her the extraordinary privilege of recognizing Him and heralding the good news of His arrival to others. A lifetime of unceasing devotion, a perpetually watchful heart, had finally found its reward. Having seen God's salvation, along with her friend Simeon, she was ready to depart in peace. Once she saw Christ's blessed little face, what more could life offer her?

But as for me, I watch in hope for the LORD, I wait for God my Savior; my God will hear me.

MICAH 7:7

LESSONS FOR OUR OWN HEARTS

Where would we be without those like Anna in the church? A few days ago my husband, Clay, performed the memorial service of a beloved ninety-year-old woman in our church. For many years Laurie Woodruff had kept a vigil of prayer for hundreds of people, not only in our church but all over the world. When Clay asked for a show of hands to indicate which ones knew Laurie had been praying for them, almost everyone in the large congregation lifted their hands. Clay informed us that while Laurie was dancing in heaven and resting from her labors, we had suffered a great loss. We needed others to step in and pick up the blazing torch of prayer that Laurie had left behind. Hers was no small ministry to the church as she labored in her prayer closet. As we scurried around doing "important" things for God, Laurie kept her faithful watch. Behind the scenes she kept apprised of needs in our lives and ministries, fought for us, and birthed fruit for us. How we will miss this precious "Anna"!

Unfortunately, there's another type of legacy in the church today, too. I am no artist, but years ago I managed to draw a cartoon with two frames. In the first frame, a man sat puzzling over a verse in his Bible. The caption was: "What I say to you, I say to everyone: 'Watch!' (Mark 13:37)." In the second frame, the same man sat in his easy chair with his soda and a contented grin, watching TV. I hate to think anyone could be that dumb when it comes to biblical interpretation. Functionally, however, it seems that many of us respond to this biblical directive in just that way.

Jesus wants us to take this matter seriously. Just look at some of

His other words in Mark 13: "Watch out that no one deceives you" (13:5); "You must be on your guard" (13:9); "So be on your guard; I have told you everything ahead of time" (13:23); "Be on guard! Be alert! You do not know when that time will come" (13:33); "Therefore keep watch because you do not know when the owner of the house will come back—whether in the evening, or at midnight, or when the rooster crows, or at dawn. If he comes suddenly, do not let him find you sleeping" (13:35-36).

Generally, passive TV-watching requires little of us. Spiritual watchfulness, on the other hand, requires an active, sustained effort. Why must we make this effort? One obvious reason is that watchfulness keeps us from falling into sin. From the context of the above Scriptures, we see that when Jesus tells us to watch, He means for us to watch for Him in anticipation of His second coming. (See also Matt. 24:42-44; 25:13; Luke 12:35-46; 21:34-36; 1 Peter 4:7.) But if we become careless, we might give in to temptation, backslide, and be unprepared to face the Lord. He specifically means for us to live a watchful life in anticipation of meeting Him when He comes.

It will shock you, but look at what happens a short chapter after Christ gave His sobering charge to His disciples. After all of His talk about watchfulness, the time had come for His core disciples to put into practice what they had heard. Knowing that His death was imminent, He took them to Gethsemane and told them, "My soul is overwhelmed with sorrow to the point of death. . . . Stay here and keep watch." Then He went off to pray. But, unlike Anna, they felt an overpowering urge to get a little shut-eye.

Soon Jesus returned to find them not watching but sleeping. "Simon," he said to Peter, "are you asleep? Could you not keep watch for one hour? Watch and pray so that you will not fall into temptation. The spirit is willing, but the body is weak." He then left them to resume praying. When He returned this second time, what did He find? His disciples sleeping again! He had no time for this, so He went off to pray some more. When He returned a third time, there they were—still sleeping! Exasperated and seeing His enemies coming, He cried to His disciples, "Are you still sleeping and resting? Enough! The hour has come. Look, the Son of Man is betrayed into the hands of sinners" (Mark 14:34, 37-41).

What a terrible way for this night to end! If only the disciples had been like Anna! How sad that they simply did not get it. If they had felt the Lord's heartbreak and passion, they might have obeyed His instructions to keep watch. Instead, they needed Solomon's admonition: "How long will you lie there, you sluggard? When will you get up from your sleep? A little sleep, a little slumber, a little folding of the hands to rest—and poverty will come on you like a bandit and scarcity like an armed man" (Prov. 6:9-11). The critical hour, like an armed bandit, took them completely by surprise.

The Lord had called His disciples to be watchmen for Him that night. In biblical times, watchmen had a duty to stand at their post, usually on the city wall, and carefully look out for anything unusual, especially danger from enemies. If someone came, they sounded a warning. This task required soberness and vigilance, especially in the late watches of the night.

Son of man, I have made you a watchman for the house of Israel; so hear the word I speak and give them warning from me.

EZEKIEL 3:17

I have posted watchmen on your walls, O Jerusalem; they will never be silent day or night. You who call on the LORD, give yourselves no rest, and give him no rest till he establishes Jerusalem and makes her the praise of the earth.

ISAIAH 62:6-7

Physical drowsiness or spiritual drowsiness—whichever it was— the disciples failed in their duty. Their enemies arrived, and the disciples fled in all directions. But thank the Lord that He did not abandon them—or us! Jesus Christ had faithfully kept His watch that night. Wrestling through His fears, He was fully prepared for what would face Him the next day. Challenging hell's gates by dying an excruciating death on the cross, He would bruise the serpent's head and set the captives free. How sad though that He had to be His own watchman and that He had no one to stand with Him during this, His most distressing hour. The disciples were spiritual slackers that night and dishonored their precious Lord for it.

We should note the opposite examples of the disciples and Anna and measure ourselves against them. If we do not dedicate ourselves to staying watchful, we easily succumb.

I will never forget the first time I heard Keith Green's song "Asleep in the Light." Clay and I were sleeping early one morning when suddenly the radio alarm clicked on. There was Keith *shouting* at us, "How can you be so dead when you've been so well fed? Jesus rose from the grave; And you! You can't even get out of bed!" Blankets went flying as we both sat bolt upright, asking, "What was that?" That morning I knew God had literally kicked us out of our comfortable bed to pray.

In Bunyan's *The Pilgrim's Progress,* the pilgrims had to journey through a particularly dangerous enemy territory called the Enchanted Ground. The atmosphere there lulls many pilgrims to sleep, never to awaken again. Surprisingly, it lies very near the end of their pilgrimage, almost to the Celestial City. Bunyan wanted to warn us that false feelings of safety can lull us, even when we feel closest to heaven. We might think that we have nearly arrived spiritually, but if we sleep on the Enchanted Ground, we might as well be an eternity away from our desired destination. How sad that so many who are nearly ready to enter the Lord's eternal kingdom and glory are dozing just outside the heavenly gates, many in front of TV sets! But not Laurie Woodruff! Not Anna!

The question for us is, "Will we keep watch with Jesus?" Like the walls upon which watchmen often stood, so the church is a walled city, God Himself providing a wall of salvation. He calls His people to stand as watchers on His wall, both to protect against enemy intrusion and also to invite His divine presence inside. If we are slacking off spiritually, we need reviving. This is no time for spiritual sloth and sleepiness, but for allegiance to duty. If we would enjoy a full reward at Christ's coming, we must renounce our drowsiness, lukewarmness, and unconcern.

And do this, understanding the present time. The hour has come for you to wake up from your slumber, because our salvation is nearer now than when we first believed. The night is nearly over; the day is almost here. So let us put aside the deeds of darkness and put on the armor of light.

ROMANS 13:11-12

Wake up! Strengthen what remains and is about to die. . . . But if you do not wake up, I will come like a thief, and you will not know at what time I will come to you.

REVELATION 3:2-3

So then, let us not be like others, who are asleep, but let us be alert and self-controlled.

1 THESSALONIANS 5:6

If you have ever been forced to heat your home with a wood-burning stove, as I have, you know the importance of watchfulness. I quickly learned how much easier it is to throw another log on a burning fire than to reignite one that has gone out. Regardless, sometimes the hassle of going outdoors for wood on a cold wintry day or night was just too much. I would put it off. Suddenly, however, the temperature indoors plummeted. I would cry, "Oh, no! I forgot to add more wood! The fire has burned out!" I would have to go out into the elements, not only to get some logs but to scrape together some kindling. Then I had to make the extra effort to get a new fire going, and I do mean extra effort. I was never good at building a fire!

The same is true of the fire in our hearts. As with the natural realm, where we maintain a fire by contributing fuel to it, so we must add fuel to our heart's watch fire. This takes some extra effort, and because it does, we can easily tire of the task and dawdle. Soon, however, we find ourselves cold and aloof toward the Lord and wondering why. Often we return to our watch fire only after some feeling of desperation drives us to it.

But look at Anna's approach. Always alert, continually watching and praying, steadfastly refusing to allow sleepiness or passivity to gain an advantage, she constantly kept her heart alive to God. No Enchanted Ground could lull her to sleep. She likely thought, *I'm almost there. How can I sleep with God's kingdom so near at hand?* Her spirit could recognize signs that others could not. Fully convinced in her heart that the Messiah would come soon, she acted in advance, constantly keeping a watchful eye out for Him, praying for His appearing, anticipating, foreseeing, expecting, believing.

We all know that spiritual leaders have a duty to keep watch. Scripture tells us that they "keep watch over you as men who must give an account" (Heb. 13:17). It commands them, "Keep watch over yourselves and all the flock of which the Holy Spirit has made you overseers" (Acts 20:28); "Watch your life and doctrine closely. Persevere in them, because if you do, you will save both yourself and your hearers" (1 Tim. 4:16). Perhaps we leave too much to our spiritual leaders though. Anna did not leave it to someone else to do her watching for her. She took the responsibility upon herself.

With much of the church today asleep and allowing heretics and hypocrites to live comfortably within its walls, how we need more Annas—faithful women who can stand the difficult tests of time, women who know the discipline of a life set apart for the Lord, women who earnestly want the traps of religion and tradition to fall off God's people, women who cannot rest until pure and undefiled worship returns to the house of God. We need women who, like Anna, keep praying, watching, waiting, and hastening the next big move of God.

I think that's exactly what the Holy Spirit wants to do in these end times—to raise up Annas, even a whole army of them—for the sake of His church and kingdom. The Lord wants women to come forth who passionately love their Lord and the church for whom He died. He wants women who not only watch their own step in this world but who intensely long for Christ's pure bride to make herself ready for His coming (Rev. 19:7). He wants His Annas to "pray in the Spirit on all occasions with all kinds of prayers and requests" and to "be alert and always keep on praying for all the saints" (Eph. 6:18). This is the time! Let the Lord's Annas arise with holy fire in their hearts!

Okay, let's come back to earth. Granted, to emulate Anna perfectly would be nearly impossible for most of us. Still, we *can* enlist in Anna's Army. Anna was not so different from everyone else. She, too, had to cultivate her watchful heart, and we can learn from her example. Here are some things Anna would tell us to do.

Live an Unencumbered Lifestyle

So many things can distract us from God's purposes. Looking at the *Amplified Bible*'s description of seed sown among thorns in Jesus' Parable of the Sower, we find a good picture of life in America today: "And the ones sown among the thorns are others who hear the Word. Then the cares and anxieties of the world, and distractions of the age, and the pleasure and delight and false glamour and deceitfulness of riches, and the craving and passionate desire for other things creep in and choke and suffocate the Word, and it becomes fruitless" (Mark 4:18-19).

Somewhere along the line, Anna had made a conscious choice of lifestyles. Having rid herself of the "thorns" of life, she successfully guarded her heart against any distractions—whether from the world, flesh, or devil—to lure her from her faithful vigil. With her heart free to respond to God alone, she cultivated a special ability to keep a faithful, watchful, perceptive eye fixed on Him and His purposes.

O my strength, I will watch for you; for you, O God, are my fortress.

PSALM 59:9 NRSV

What about us? While much in our lives seems beyond our control, we still have many options. Is the house with the huge payment really necessary? What about the new car, boat, latest technological gadgetry, fancy vacation?

A young newlywed couple came in one day for counseling. Marital bliss had quickly given way to constant warfare. God was somewhere far away, and they couldn't seem to contact Him. While it was not obvious to them, their problem was easy for Clay and me to discern. After their wedding, they had laid aside their pure devotion to Christ in favor of worldly images of happiness and success. These false values had so bombarded and seduced their senses that they had charged many thousands of dollars worth of new furniture on charge cards. Now the bitter fruit of their staggering debt was eating them alive. We counseled them to return the furniture immediately and get out of debt. Their mistake nearly cost them their marriage and, worse, their walk with Christ.

So it is with more than a few of us. Jesus said, "Take care! Be on your guard against all kinds of greed; for one's life does not consist in the abundance of possessions" (Luke 12:15 NRSV). He went on to warn us against the error of being rich in possessions and impoverished toward God (Luke 12:16-21). Truly, it is the rare soul who can be rich toward both. If we sincerely ask God for hearts like Anna's, we will surely hear Him calling us to simplify our lifestyle.

Culturally, we are such a busy and preoccupied people. Just assembling, maintaining, using, and paying for all that stuff we keep accumulating is enough to bury us. But then we must also cope with avalanching time commitments that add to our exhaustion. Even our children are trying to cope with the stress of their busy schedules! Who is to blame? You, along with many others, might protest your innocence. I can almost hear some of you cry, "Wait a minute! I've got God-given responsibilities, and because of them, I am not free like Anna." True, but whether we suffer under a tyrannical schedule, debts that seem as impossible as the national one, or a host of unimportant time bandits, more often than not we have become victims of our own misguided choices.

God wants to train you to discern the difference between what is necessary and what distracts from His purposes for your life. He wants to remove the tangle of spiritual "thorns" choking your spiritual (and even your mental, physical, and emotional) life. If you let Him, He will show you how to cultivate a watchful heart so you can keep a resolute focus even in the busiest and most trying of times.

I wait for the LORD, my soul waits, and in his word I put my hope.
My soul waits for the Lord more than watchmen wait for the morning, more than watchmen wait for the morning.

PSALM 130:5-6

Avoid Empty Religion

Besides the more obvious distractions from living a watchful Christian life, a minefield of religious ones can draw our hearts away. The religious rulers of Anna's day fasted often and made lengthy prayers. They seemed alert and watchful. Yet, unlike Anna, their eyes and hearts were focused in the wrong places. God had called them to keep their lives bound up in Him, fixing their hearts on His purposes, looking for His revelation. Instead, they had become permanently focused on themselves and what others thought of them. Their own egos seduced their hearts away from true devotion to God. Their sole preoccupation was with a religious system that fed their pride and self-righteousness. Even if they had overheard Anna that day excitedly prophesying the good news, they were too busy being religious to care. Long since, they had lost interest in keeping a faithful watch. They were so very near and yet so very far from the kingdom. The Savior of the world visited right under their noses, and while Anna noticed, they were oblivious.

Look at the disciples again, this time as Jesus leads them through the temple. No longer the cooing Christ child adored by Anna, He was there that day as the Lord of the temple. But the disciples missed it. Instead, enamored with the temple's grandeur, they exclaimed, "Look, teacher! What massive stones! What magnificent buildings!" Unimpressed with these religious trappings, Jesus replied flatly that the whole thing would be torn down (Mark 13:1-2; Luke 21:5-6). This shocked them. As soon as they could get Him alone, several of them asked when these things would take place. But Jesus had little interest in the "when" of it all. His uppermost concern was "how" they might respond to this perilous time. Forewarning them, He said, "Watch out that no one deceives you" (Mark 13:5; Luke 21:8).

Look again at Anna. Luke calls her a prophetess—the only one in the New Testament besides Philip's four daughters (Acts 21:9) and a false prophetess whom Christ calls "Jezebel" (Rev. 2:20). Obviously, as a genuine prophetess of the Lord, Anna never let religious trappings sidetrack her watchful heart.

And the lookout shouted, "Day after day, my lord, I stand on the watchtower; every night I stay at my post."

ISAIAH 21:8

On my bed I remember you; I think of you through the watches of the night.

PSALM 63:6

Don't Excuse Yourself from Your Duty

So what are your excuses for spiritual inactivity and evasion? How have you managed to exempt yourself? However you justify it, I think Anna might have had better reason. If she had looked for excuses to give up her watch, she could have easily found any number of them. She had many reasons to shed bitter tears. She had no husband, no children, no apparent means of support. As a poor widow, she was of an economically and socially disadvantaged class. In those times especially widows could live lonely, unhappy, destitute lives. Any other situation would have been preferable.

But Anna is not described as lonely, bitter, deprived, or incapacitated. As a young childless widow, her hope didn't go to the grave with her husband. She never let demanding, self-pitying complaints to God or society overcome her. During a time that otherwise might have spelled despondency and despair, she drew close to God and let Him give her back a reason for living. He healed her grief and met her in her loneliness. Fervency and devotion grew until her relationship with her divine "Husband" became so intimate and personal that she could spend all her hours with Him, serving Him in the temple.

Besides the difficulties related to widowhood, let's not forget the issue of Anna's age. She was very old, about as old as anyone can get. She could have looked at her dilapidated body and whined, "I'm just not good for anything anymore." But in her mind, fruitful service related little to age. Her body might be old and shriveled, but her best years were never behind her. Never old enough to know better, she had no intention of retiring from God's work.

Can't you see her there, faithfully waiting on God for years on end, never idle, never disheartened, never retiring from God's service, always hoping in the promise, pressing in and pressing on, keeping her senses keenly attuned to God's Spirit? Can you imagine this faithful prophetess ever backing off and saying to the young folk, "I've put in my time; now it's your turn"? For many of us, however, the light goes out as old age marches on.

Grandma Floodberg was an elderly widow, who, at more than eighty years old, had swollen legs nearly too weak to support her. She was so miserably sad and felt useless. Clay advised her to develop her prayer life and reminded her of her children, her grandchildren, and great-grandchildren who so desperately needed her prayers. So she began her prayer ministry. Day by day as she let God show her how best to pray, her sad countenance was transformed and took on a happy glow.

I also think of Mama Ginia, my mother-in-law (mother-in-love, she says). A source of great blessing and strength in our lives, she greets each new dawn by poring over her prayer list. She prays for us; she prays for her church; she prays for everyone she knows. The years fly by, the pages turn yellow, the list gets longer—but this dear woman just keeps watching and praying. Prayer is not the only expression of her faithful watch, however. For as long as I have known her—thirty wonderful years—her watchful heart has looked enthusiastically to the Holy Spirit to guide her in acts of service for His glory. She may be over eighty, but she has the heart of a young woman.

God's people never retire. Old folk have so much to contribute. Those who are wise realize that no matter what their limitations, God can still use them if they make themselves available. They can testify boldly, "Therefore we do not lose heart. Though outwardly we are wasting away, yet inwardly we are being renewed day by day" (2 Cor. 4:16). How encouraging it is to the rest of us to know those who, through long lives of dedication and sacrifice, remain true to the Lord's call. Their gray heads are honorable because of the enduring and endearing example they leave behind them. How blessed they are when they pass away into glory!

Let the Annas of God arise! Let them rise out of obscurity and take their rightful places in God's kingdom!

They will still bear fruit in old age, they will stay fresh and green, proclaiming, "The LORD is upright; he is my Rock, and there is no wickedness in him."

PSALM 92:14-15

Let the Watch Fire of Your Faith Burn Strong

Perhaps so many of us need to be reminded, "Turn your eyes upon Jesus," because we have carelessly failed to "fix our eyes on Jesus" (Heb. 12:2). Unable to stay spiritually focused, we fix our eyes everywhere else. Thus we have no idea how to get an unshakable, unquenchable spiritual watch fire going.

But we had better learn, if not purely for the Lord, then at least for our own sakes. For God's Word warns, "We must pay more careful attention, therefore, to what we have heard, so that we do not drift away" (Heb. 2:1); "Be self-controlled and alert. Your enemy the devil prowls around like a roaring lion looking for someone to devour" (1 Peter 5:8); "Watch out that you do not lose what you have worked for, but that you may be rewarded fully" (2 John 8).

So how can we keep spiritual purpose alive in our hearts? So many of God's daughters run around looking for the fresh wind, the new revelation, the next wave of exciting spiritual manifestations. Anna's life may seem boring to them—the same old stuff. It was not the same old stuff to Anna though, and it is not the same old stuff to anyone who fights through to burning faith and purpose. Perceiving God's promises in the process of fulfillment, Anna watched for the Lord tirelessly. As the years progressed, how could she miss noticing her own body's decline? Yet she never thought, *I'd better take care of myself.* Instead, she thought, *I'd better take care of the Lord's business.*

Anna devoted herself to the spiritual disciplines. Wanting to serve the Lord more effectively on her watch, she controlled her fleshly appetites by fasting. Wanting to receive further revelations from the Lord, she let go of creature comforts by filling her days with prayer. She was undoubtedly one of "his chosen ones, who cry out to him day and night" (Luke 18:7). Yet her prayers were not for her own interests but for God's. She had truly offered her body "as a living sacrifice, holy and acceptable to God" (Rom. 12:1 NRSV).

Naturally, most of us cannot pray and fast all the time. We can, however, learn to pray habitually as we go about the affairs of our

day. We can make prayer our life and our life a prayer. "Devote yourselves to prayer," says God's Word, "being watchful and thankful"
(Col. 4:2).

We can also be sure that throughout her long and devoted life,
Anna had saturated her mind and heart with God's Word. She obviously knew all the Old Testament prophecies concerning the
Messiah, and at some point the Holy Spirit convinced her that the
time was near.

Not only did Anna fuel her watch fire with fasting, praying, and
meditating on God's Word, but she always made sure she was at the
right place at the right time. Staying closest to where she expected to
see God act, she never needed to go to church. She already lived
there. What about us? How often is our seat in church left empty?
Over the years, multitudes of young couples had come to the temple
to dedicate their infants to the Lord. How many times did Anna, with
her watchful heart, stand by and pray, "Lord, is this the one?"

This dear, little lady, who had already found such enrichment in
keeping her long and faithful watch, received an extra special blessing on that day. It was no coincidence that she approached Mary and
Joseph in the temple "at that very moment" (Luke 2:38). After all,
she had been there day and night, watching and praying—though He
seemed to tarry—year in and year out, believing He would come.
Her daily, constant, faithful vigil had finally paid off. "Blessed are the
pure in heart," Jesus would later promise, "for they will see God"
(Matt. 5:8). Gazing into those tiny eyes, Anna got to "see God"—
God-in-flesh, the divine King of kings and Lord of lords. What a
moment!

Anna was a model of the elevated position women enjoy under
the New Covenant. An intercessor of the first rank, she faithfully
"prayed without ceasing" (1 Thess. 5:17 NRSV). She is included in the
long line of prophets and prophetesses who throughout the genera-
tions heralded the coming Messiah. The others, however, never laid
eyes on Him. Not only did Anna enjoy this unique privilege, but she

got to meet the parents. Simeon's prophetic word to Mary about a sword piercing her soul must have troubled the young mother deeply. But God used Anna's exuberant prophetic testimonial to gladden her trembling heart.

Not only that, but Anna had the joyful privilege of announcing the Messiah's arrival. Her discernment was so sharp that she knew who the babe was. Blazoning the news "to all who were looking forward to the redemption of Jerusalem" (Luke 2:38), Anna was more than a prophetess. Along with the shepherds who proclaimed Christ's birth, she can appropriately be considered an early Christian missionary.

How many revelations, how many visitations, how many moves of God's Spirit do we miss because, otherwise preoccupied, we simply lose sight of our spiritual purpose? Anna would soon die. What if she had given in to some distraction and simply stayed away on that blessed day? It was, after all, an otherwise ordinary day in a very long lifetime. Fortunately, wisdom had taught her that the hour of visitation cannot catch off guard those who faithfully maintain their spiritual watch fires. Immortalized in God's holy Word, Anna is a testimony to us all of the awesome blessings that God bestows on watchful hearts.

Have you tired of your watch? Perhaps you are young, or you may be old. Either way, you may feel like a burned-out has-been. Weary of your duty and giving up in disillusioned frustration, you have allowed the devil to steal your hope somehow. But I have good news for you, weary heart! Renewal is yours! Just follow Anna, and let your heart return to its watch fire! He will surely visit you, pouring the renewing oil of His grace on you. He will enable you to wake up and hope on. He will give you the fresh fire you need.

Will you do it? Will you enlist or reenlist in Anna's Army? By His grace, will you carry on faithfully in your duty—watching, waiting, seeking, praising? The world is slipping into deeper and deeper darkness. It's happening on our watch. The Lord has strategies for us; He has an anointing for us. He wants to make us shining beacons in the night, pointing the way for His lost world. This is a battle we must win.

One church I recently read about (All Nations Church in Charlotte, North Carolina) has what they call a "Watch of the Lord" service for eight hours each Friday night. Beginning their "watch" at 10 P.M., they fast and pray and listen to the Lord. Eight hours later— at 6 A.M.—they close with Communion. Reportedly, this is no heavy yoke to them but an exciting, joyful experience. What an army of Annas the Lord has in that church!

Jesus will come soon. He tells us, "Be on guard! Be alert! You do not know when that time will come" (Mark 13:33). It's time to take Him seriously. Stop slumbering! Wake up! Hope on! Carry on! Get ready—"WATCH!"

Anna prepared well for Christ's first coming. She knew the signs to watch for. What joyful anticipation filled her heart. We must be ready for His second coming and help prepare others as well. We should live each day as if He might come this day. We should live each day as if it might be our last one here. We should be faithful every day. The time is short. Soon and very soon we will see the Lord—this time riding on the clouds of glory! What joy this should give us!

See, I am coming like a thief! Blessed is the one who stays awake and is clothed, not going about naked and exposed to shame.

REVELATION 16:15 NRSV

Listen! Your watchmen lift up their voices; together they shout for joy. When the LORD returns to Zion, they will see it with their own eyes.

ISAIAH 52:8

Heart Check

1. As you examine your heart, do you relate better to the sleepy disciples or to watchful Anna?

2. What distracting influences are quenching your spiritual watch-fire?

3. What steps can you now take to cultivate a more watchful heart?

4. What is the most important thing you can apply to your life from Anna's example?

5. Compose a prayer to God in response to this chapter's truths.

2

The Syrophoenician Woman

THE TENACIOUS HEART

MATTHEW 15:21-28; MARK 7:24-30

MY GODS ARE WORTHLESS! They don't heal; they don't deliver; they don't comfort or give me hope. They're good for nothing! The Syrophoenician woman had had enough. Now running behind the band of weary Jews, she knew what she wanted, and she let everyone know it. She wanted to talk to the man in their midst, whom they were trying to protect—the famous Rabbi, Jesus of Nazareth. As she followed close behind, crying and pleading for mercy, they tried hard to ignore her.

Did they think that by surrounding their Master, they could keep her from Him? They were mistaken. You see, this woman was a mother whose heart was breaking for a daughter in desperate need. So she would not take their "hint." Going home empty-handed was not an option. Therefore, we call this woman's heart The Tenacious Heart. And she would need tenacity, for she faced serious testing this day.

This story really begins with Jesus looking for solitude. Following an intense season of ministry on both sides of the Sea of Galilee, He told His disciples, "Come with me by yourselves to a quiet place and get some rest" (Mark 6:31). But whenever they tried to get away, a huge crowd followed them. After miraculously feeding more than five thousand of their number, Jesus and His followers crossed to the northwest side of the lake. This took them to the lovely plain of Gennesaret, but they would find no rest there either. Word spread like wildfire that they had come, and Jesus healed a host of their sick people. Adding to this pressure, a group of religious leaders interrupted His ministry, having come some eighty miles from Jerusalem just to wrangle with Him. After a heated dispute over what is clean and unclean (Matt. 14:34—15:1ff.; Mark 6:53—7:1ff.), He was intent on finding that elusive place of solitude He longed for.

Withdrawing from Jewish territory altogether, Jesus led His disciples into the neighboring Gentile country of Phoenicia. They had traveled some thirty-five miles when they arrived at the outskirts of the ancient coastal city of Tyre on the Mediterranean Sea. We see no indication that He intended to preach or do miracles in that region. Exhausted from His ministry and from this latest journey, He looked for seclusion. But His fame followed Him and preceded Him. He could not hide.

Meanwhile, the distressed Syrophoenician woman, a local resident, was looking for answers. The condition with which her precious daughter suffered was no light affliction. It was so serious that it seemed it might kill her at any time. You see, a malicious evil spirit tormented the child, and half the time she was out of her mind and the other half out of control.

How this brokenhearted mother longed to see her daughter's dancing eyes, innocent laugh, and sweet personality again. Crying herself to sleep each night, the mother awakened every morning to a recurring dark and fearsome nightmare, one that never faded but only grew worse. The dreadful, eerie alien bedeviling her child grew stronger, not weaker. Trembling, the mother would wonder, *What will this day bring?*

Then it would happen—again! Her rapidly graying hair would suddenly stand on end as the hideous demon manifested. Horrified and helpless, she looked on as her beloved child's face twisted and distorted, her body writhed and contorted, her voice deepened, her mouth foamed, and she broke into paroxysms of laughter—spitting, cursing, or shrieking. Would the young victim wound herself this time, self-destructively yanking at her hair, poking and beating herself, or worse? Would she turn vicious—hitting, kicking, biting, and tearing the house apart? Would she suddenly turn and attack her mother, the neighbor's dog, or other children? The woman had tried to restrain her, but it was useless. The girl's strength during these fits was at least twice her own.

Living in Tyre, surrounded by her pagan culture, this woman did not know much about the true and living God. Yet she had heard of Jesus Christ. Many from Tyre and Sidon had traveled south to see Him (Mark 3:8; Luke 6:17), and they always came home with marvelous reports of healings and deliverances from demonic bondage. At first she had raised her eyebrows with interest at the stories but thought, *He's a Jew. He'll do nothing for me.* That was then, however; now she was far more desperate.

She had given up trying to appease the demon, and her prayers were having no effect. She had given up the large repertoire of incantations, charms, and rituals suggested to her. There was no use trying to pacify her daughter's fears, to persuade her to resist her impulses, or to convince her to behave like other children. Nothing worked against the diabolical power. All she tried had failed.

The poor woman was worn out—weary of the demon, weary of her own inability to cope with it, weary of caring for her daughter night and day, weary of being on pins and needles, weary of neighbors who shunned them. This was a fate worse than death, and it had gone on way too long. She didn't know which way to turn, but she had to find help.

Then she heard some incredible news, so wonderful that it made her heart leap. Jesus of Nazareth, the very one reputed to cast demons out with a word, was coming toward town! *The Jewish miracle-worker is coming here? This is it! I know this is it!* No sooner had word reached her ear than she was tearing down the road to meet Him. Hope blazed in her heart as she thought of all the stories she had heard of His compassionate and powerful healing wonders. Suddenly she spotted a group coming up the road. There they were—Jesus and His disciples! Full of expectation, she hurried toward them, hoping He would help her.

But would He? We might assume that, as was His habit, He would immediately meet her request. But this time it would not be so easy. The woman's nationality was about to become an issue. Her home of Tyre was only fifty miles from Galilee, but with Greek influences dominating it and Gentiles almost exclusively populating it, Tyre was a world away culturally.

Matthew calls this woman "a Canaanite," and Mark calls her "a Greek, born in Syrian Phoenicia." Matthew's Jewish readers knew the Canaanites as the Baal-worshiping archenemies of Israel when God's people settled into the Promised Land. Descendants of Noah's grandson Canaan, whom Noah had cursed (Gen. 9:25), the Canaanites were the most morally despised of Israel's enemies in the Old Testament, and Jews still viewed them as unworthy of God's blessings.

Mark, on the other hand, writing to Gentile Christians in Rome, enabled them easily to identify the part of the empire that was her home: She was a Greek (a Gentile) and a Syrophoenician (her country of Phoenicia belonged to the Roman province of Syria). In any case, there was no love lost between Jews and Canaanite Syrophoenicians. As for the historic Canaanite cities of Tyre and Sidon, they were notoriously wicked. To make a point, Jesus would later say, "But I tell you, it will be more bearable for Tyre and Sidon on the day of judgment than for you" (Matt. 11:22).

The woman understood the issues. She knew she was an outsider, undeserving of God's mercy. So as she approached the band of travelers, she began to call to Jesus from some distance, not daring to get too close lest she offend Him. "Lord, Son of David," she cried, "have mercy on me!" Despite the fact that she was by culture a Greek and by religion a pagan, she had acknowledged both Jesus' authority and His deity. Calling Him "Lord" (Greek *kurios*), a royal title, she identified Him as Israel's sovereign king. Calling Him "Son of David," a messianic title, she identified Him as the Jewish Messiah.

But Jesus didn't seem impressed. He just kept walking, and His disciples drew in tighter about Him as if to form a shield. The disciples did not yet know that she had a tenacious heart. Out of patience and disregarding proprieties, she began to call out more earnestly. Pouring out her sad story, she cried, "My daughter is suffering terribly from demon-possession" (Matt. 15:22). She could not, however, seem to get Jesus' attention.

This was an unexpected setback. Jesus and His disciples were giving her the cold shoulder, brushing her off, snubbing her. She wasn't sure how to respond, but however the situation made her feel, it didn't deter her for a moment. *The demon has my beloved child,* she thought, *but I will get her back if it kills me! I can't give up; I won't give up!*

Knowing Jesus was her only hope, her tenacious heart moved her to press on, crying all the louder, "Have mercy on me!" Over and over, she begged and pleaded, "Have mercy on me!" If she had heard that Jesus was just there to enjoy a private time of fellowship with His disciples, she didn't care. But the healer would not cooperate. Not only did He refuse to answer her prayer, but he "did not answer a word" (Matt. 15:23). Nowhere in the Gospels do we see Jesus brush off someone's need as He did here.

Since she had already suffered unspeakable torment, she must have thought, *What's a little more?* So she kept on pestering Him. So persistent, so annoying, so unwilling to concede defeat was she that she completely frustrated the disciples. At their wits' end, they could see that ignoring her was solving nothing.

Feeling specially chosen by God, the disciples of Jesus at this time were deeply nationalistic and smug Jewish men. Interpreting their Master's behavior to mean that this despised and troublesome Gentile woman annoyed Him, too, they were only too happy to share in His seeming rebuff. "Send her away," they begged, "for she keeps crying out after us" (Matt. 15:23).

But Jesus had reasons for letting this go on. They had no regard for this woman's great love for her suffering daughter. Neither could they respect the great courage it took for her to run after Jesus and persist, despite who she was and how she was being treated. To them she was a nobody, far removed from the promises and blessings of God. *Why, they thought, should our Master show favor to this galling foreigner?*

Seeming to agree that they should send her away, Jesus answered them, "I was sent only to the lost sheep of Israel" (Matt. 15:24). Evidently He said this to emphasize that He should restrict His brief earthly activities as the Messiah to God's chosen people, "the lost sheep of Israel." The privileges of God's kingdom were for God's people. For that reason, He could not be at everyone else's beck and call, however urgent their requests. Whatever His reason, however, it sounded very much as if He intended to chase the woman away. This must have satisfied the disciples. To the poor woman, however, it meant another no.

Wouldn't she now be altogether discouraged? Not only had He not answered her request, but He had argued against helping her. She was a lost sheep, all right, but not one from the house of Israel. Case closed? Hardly. This woman remained undaunted even when her prospects for success seemed to get more bleak. Mark's Gospel relates that Jesus entered a house. Clearly, he wanted to disappear behind closed doors before crowds could gather. Perhaps He had looked forward to resting in this hospitable home. The thought of His host washing His feet and His hostess bringing Him a hot meal no doubt was in His mind. As a human, He needed time to shut out the demands of His ministry and relax with His disciples.

Would the woman finally get the message and go home, or would she linger outside the door, crying pitifully? Neither. She would gladly keep risking their anger by making herself a nuisance. There was simply too much at stake for her to give up. So, to everyone's amazement, she boldly followed the invited guests right inside the house. Shamelessly thrusting her way past the disciples, she fell at the feet of Jesus. Using a Greek word for worship, *proskuneo,* Matthew indicates that this was an act of worship. The King James Version concurs: "Then came she and worshipped him . . ." (Matt. 15:25). Next with all the earnestness in her heart, she cried, "Lord, help me!" (Matt. 15:25).

She had flung herself upon His mercy, and now she had His full attention. What would He do? She held her breath and waited. For the first time He addressed her: "First let the children eat all they want," He told her, "for it is not right to take the children's bread and toss it to their dogs" (Mark 7:27). Ouch! How could He speak to her in this way? Sometimes He spoke roughly to religious hypocrites, but she was a poor desperate woman. Was it because she was simply a stranger to the covenant? Tension filled the air. Now what would she do? The disciples must have wondered, *What is it about no that this woman doesn't understand?*

When used in Greek or Jewish culture, "dog" was not a friendly term. Applying it to someone was a sign of dishonor and contempt. Jews commonly applied it to Gentiles since they thought Gentiles no more likely than dogs to receive God's blessing. Most people, therefore, would feel stung and deeply offended if so branded. It is a wonder the woman didn't storm away. "Is this the one so renowned for His compassionate care?" she might have shouted. "I should have stayed home!"

How could Jesus say such a shocking thing? Actually His label was not so insulting as it might seem. Rather than choosing the term typically used for a dog (Greek *kuon*), which could describe the wild dogs of the streets, he used another word. In its only New Testament usage, Jesus chose a word for a small dog or puppy, basically a small family pet (Greek *kunarion*). Still, this was not the kind of reply the woman would have hoped for. It seems out of character for Jesus to respond this way.

Was Jesus showing bigotry? Of course not. Anyone who truly

knows Jesus recognizes that He was not racially prejudiced. This was not the first Gentile to whom he had shown mercy. When crowds came from the Decapolis, a league of ten Gentile cities, Jesus healed these people right along with the Jews (Matt. 4:24-25). In fact, He ministered to Gentiles on many occasions, including the woman at the well (John 4:7-42), a centurion (Matt. 8:5-13), and a leper who came back and thanked Him (Luke 17:11-19). He even told a parable of a benevolent Samaritan (Luke 10:30-37). No, He was definitely not bigoted. Besides, He would never contradict the truth that God wants to reach everyone (Ps. 22:27; Isa. 56:7; Matt. 28:19).

Was He then indicating that this particular woman had become an unbearable nuisance to Him? Hardly. He always seemed ready to minister to people's needs. This was the case with Jairus (Mark 5:22-43; Luke 8:41-56), the widow of Nain (Luke 7:11-16), a crippled woman (Luke 13:10-17), and a host of others (Matt. 9:35).

Since the Jesus we know and love never treated anyone's need with callous disregard, it is likely for several reasons that He saw a special opportunity here. First, He believed strongly that while His ministry ultimately was to all people, His immediate mission was primarily to "the lost sheep of Israel." He would indeed be a "light to the Gentiles," but the time was not yet. This is why He sent His disciples out, restricting their ministry to the Jews (Matt. 10:5-6). Jews were to have the first opportunity to accept Him as their Messiah since they were to present the truth of salvation to the world. So He told the woman that His first priority was to provide food for the children and not allow pets to interrupt the family meal.

Second, He may have seen an excellent opportunity for instructing His disciples about the universality of His kingdom, that faith is available to all people. Were they still racists who thought themselves the exclusive objects of God's favor? He would test their hearts by using the word *dog*, which reflected the Jewish attitude, to contrast it with His own view. He wanted them to learn that God extends His blessing to all people, that He seeks to save not just a few, but as many as possible, and that He had chosen them to spread this good news.

Finally, Jesus was doing a special work in the woman. Those whom Christ most intends to honor, He sometimes lays low with a sense of their own unworthiness. A Gentile stranger to the Jewish law and covenants, she had to realize that her only hope lay in the Jewish Messiah's grace and mercy. He knew what was in her heart, the strength of her faith, and her ability, by His grace, to break through disheartening obstacles. So He tested her with words that struck a blow to her pride. Far from begrudging His blessings, He was drawing from her heart the deep and rich deposits of faith. His testing of her made her heart all the more tenacious to receive the help she needed.

While most would have felt defeated by now, she did not let this further denial crush her. In fact, rather than seeing the door slammed shut, she saw the Son of David holding it open to her. She even saw a bright shard of sunlight coming through that open door. His words, "Let the children first be fed," led her to expect that her turn would come, that He still had something for her.

She knew that as a heathen woman, unclean in Jewish eyes and viewed as a dog, she should not argue this point. Neither should she dispute to whom Christ was sent. She understood His theological reluctance to honor her needs over His own people's and would refrain from making self-justifying claims that she was as good as anyone else. Instead, she argued on other grounds, using to her advantage His very theological argument. Proving herself a genuine Greek (Greeks had a talent for making witty and spirited comebacks), she artfully replied, "Yes, Lord; yet even the dogs under the table eat the children's crumbs" (Mark 7:28 ESV).

In essence she said, "Yes, Lord, You must feed Your children first. I'm just an unworthy Gentile who wouldn't dare begrudge the Jews their rightful portion. Go ahead—serve them well. But please remember that even the household pets under the table get to lick up the crumbs. Answering my request surely will deprive no one of his share. Please, Lord, I'm willing to be fed, if only by Your crumbs."

If she saw no smile in the Lord's eyes before this, she surely did now. Her remarkable courage, her love for her child, her humility, her tenacious heart, and now her quick and brilliant response drew His admiration. Seeming to do a complete turnabout, He declared for everyone to hear, "Woman, you have great faith!" (Matt. 15:28) .

He had just commended her in a way He had never commended one of His own disciples. In fact, only days before, He had scolded Peter for his lack of faith, saying, "You of little faith, why did you doubt?" (Matt. 14:31). Peter had courageously stepped out of a boat with faith that the other disciples did not have. But his faith fell apart as soon as he took his eyes off Jesus and focused instead on the wind and waves. But here was this woman with a tenacious heart who refused to permit unfavorable circumstances to quench her fire or redirect her focus. And Jesus praised her. Just think of what Peter and the other disciples learned from her this day.

Not only did this pagan Gentile woman win a rare commendation from Christ, but she finally got what she came for—the joy of hearing Him say the four precious words that she had so desperately longed to hear: "Your request is granted" (Matt. 15:28). Filled with joy and gratitude, she got up and ran home as quickly as her feet would carry her. This wonderful mother, who would stop at nothing to obtain God's blessing for her daughter, was no doubt met at her door with a delightful scene. Gone were the oppression and darkness in her home, and there was her darling daughter in her right mind, giggling, dancing—free at last.

As for this Syrophoenician woman, she now knew from her own experience the power, mercy, and truth of Jesus Christ. Things would never again be the same for her. She had learned for a certainty that it is better to feed on the "crumbs" of truth than on the loaves of false-hood. Her home, her very heart, and her life were infused with God's light. Proving in the end that God's concern extends beyond Israel, she may have been one of Christ's first Gentile converts. As a believer, she would no longer see herself as a dog. Yes, Jesus had cleansed her daughter of a demon, but He had cleansed the mother of her stigma. Rather than eating crumbs on the floor, she was now an honored member of the family at Christ's glorious table of grace.

LESSONS FOR OUR OWN HEARTS

Is there an artist, a musician, or a preacher in history who has portrayed Christ with His back to a needy soul? No, and that is because we are hard pressed ever to find Him behaving in an uninviting or ungracious way. He always seemed to respond immediately to human need. Yet here we have Him turning His back to this suffering Syrophoenician woman, withholding His power from her. What was He doing? He was teaching lessons to her, to His disciples, and to all who would hear this story. We can learn many things from the Syrophoenician woman's encounter with Christ, but perhaps the blessing of her tenacious heart is the greatest. A tenacious heart, one that holds persistently to its belief or goal, kept her pursuing Jesus until she saw her prayer answered. As it played prominently in her victory, such a heart is also a key to our experiencing a victorious Christian life.

Karen Loritts, in *A Mother's Legacy,* speaks of her mother's tenacious heart: "Mom had tenacity—a real fighter's spirit. . . ." Through long years of raising her children in a government housing project, this single mom had worked hard both to provide for her family and to instill in them values of godliness and responsibility. In the end, her grateful daughter declares, "Mom's tenacity, hard work, and endurance paid off."[1] What greater triumph is there than to have your children arise and call you blessed (Prov. 31:28).

How can we develop a tenacious heart that overcomes discouraging setbacks and obstacles—a heart that refuses to give up, that is firmly committed to "press on toward the goal to win the prize" (Phil. 3:14)? Here are some important considerations.

What We Should Believe About the Lord

All of us go through stress and pain when we do not see God answering our prayers. But things are not always as they seem. Often before God does a work for us, He does a work in us. Just look at this woman. Her tenacity was born of desperation. Her daughter's demonic affliction had caused this mother unspeakable pain. In seeking solutions, however, her heart's tenacity grew. Finally, with other resources exhausted, she came to see Jesus as her only hope. She became a woman of firm belief, but her convictions soon got tested. Would she give up? Jesus drew out of her a boldness she had not known before, a zealously tenacious heart. She knew that Jesus had a blessing for her that was worth fighting for. She would rather taste crumbs from His table than swallow her culture's false hopes any longer.

Perhaps in this story God is telling us that to receive the blessing, it takes dogged faith in Him and in Him alone. It means seeing the world's open doors as closed and God's closed doors as open. Perhaps it seems that God is not listening, that by all appearances, we will never receive our blessing or achieve our goal. But we must believe in the Lord—that He is the only hope; that He is all-sufficient; that His love, grace, and mercy will not fail; that even when He seems to have turned his back on us, He still remains our best and most trust-worthy Friend. No matter what, we must believe that in the end God will prove His concern for us, that He always hears and will answer our prayers in His own best time and way. When relentless troubles barrage us, we must believe that He has not abandoned us; when formidable challenges confront us, we must believe that He is with us; when the problems of our loved ones, our church, or our nation seem insurmountable, we must believe that He hears our prayers of intercession and is working through them.

The Syrophoenician woman's faith was tested with God's silence (Matt. 15:23) and with God's refusal (Matt. 15:24). But having received a God-given vision, she locked onto it, believing for the

God-given result. That day her tenacious heart overcame every obstacle—misunderstanding, rejection, humiliation, and denial. Indeed, it wrought a resounding victory. And we have so much more reason to believe than she did! She did not have His Word; she did not have His promises; she did not know about the cross; she did not see the big picture. We do. If we want a tenacious heart that wins spiritual victories, we must believe in the Lord. He urges us, "Believe in God, believe also in me" (John 14:1 NRSV).

What We Should Believe About Ourselves

When the Syrophoenician woman came bursting in on their privacy, the disciples saw nothing but a troublesome foreigner. Since Joshua's conquest of Canaan, Jews regarded such pagan people as a corrupting influence (Ezra 9:1). But the Savior of the world was not in the business of throwing people away. He had met the needs of many Gentiles without concern for their place of birth or religious heritage. But He was testing this woman's tenacious heart. This was a woman who had been sufficiently humbled. The disciples probably thought that anyone with even an ounce of self-respect would not carry on as she did. Not only did she make a scene as she followed them, but she burst through the door uninvited. Not only did she accept the label of "dog," but she would gladly feed on the "crumbs" of God's kingdom.

Nevertheless, despite her genuine humility, this woman believed she could convince Christ to answer her prayer. He seemed to make an issue of who *she* was, but she had faith in who *He* was. She might have heard how He had offended His own people by reminding them of Elijah's mission to the Gentile widow of Zarephath, not fifteen miles from Tyre. (See Luke 4:25-26. You can read about the Widow of Zarephath, a woman with a Crisis-stricken Heart, in *Healing for the Heart*, the second book in this series.) If the Syrophoenician woman had heard this and other stories, she had no trouble believing He was the merciful, gracious, loving, and yet powerful Messiah. Her strong faith enabled her to approach Him boldly and persuasively. She believed she could pass the barricades and enter the circle of His grace, laying hold on the blessing her daughter so desperately needed.

This woman puts most of us to shame. We have so many advantages over her, so many more reasons to pray with confidence. Not only do we know Christ as our sovereign Lord, but we have a position of privilege in Him that she had no right to claim. As a Syrophoenician, she could not justifiably call herself one of His own. But we can. If we have come to Christ in faith, receiving His saving grace, we are "no longer foreigners and aliens, but fellow citizens with God's people and members of God's household" (Eph. 2:19). That makes us heirs!

Too often people have a problem with how they see themselves. True, most people have a pride problem, and many deprive themselves of spiritual blessings simply because they are so proud. But perhaps more common are the feelings of unworthiness that greatly hinder their spiritual progress.

There was a long stage in my Christian life when I shrank back from receiving Christ's blessing simply because of my own feelings of unworthiness. Then I woke up one day to the fact that I had spent years under the Master's table when all along He had reserved a seat for me at His table. How tragic that I occupied myself with licking up the crumbs below when I could have been feasting on the whole loaf above! Might I ask how many of you behave similarly?

He who did not spare his own Son, but gave him up for us all—how will he not also, along with him, graciously give us all things?

ROMANS 8:32

Perhaps we are so willing to settle for crumbs because we still see ourselves as unacceptable "dogs" in the kingdom. But Jesus does not see us that way, and He doesn't want us to be content with crumbs. He does want us to have humble hearts that gratefully take the lowest seat at the table (Luke 14:7-11). But God has "raised us up with Christ and seated us with him in the heavenly realms in Christ Jesus" (Eph. 2:6), and He wants us to enjoy the full benefits of the feast. We are at His table. We must not settle for crumbs.

The Lord asks, "Which of you, if his son asks for bread, will give him a stone? . . . If you, then, though you are evil, know how to give good gifts to your children, how much more will your Father in heaven give good gifts to those who ask him!" (Matt. 7:9, 11). He also assures us, " . . . how much more will your Father in heaven give the Holy Spirit to those who ask him!" (Luke 11:13). The living Bread of Life does not want us to settle for the Holy Spirit's crumbs but for His fullness.

While I sat on the floor, Christ kept looking under the table and calling, "Come and dine!" (John 21:12 KJV). But the devil would argue, "No! Stay on the floor where you belong, you dog!" Who was I going to believe? It was my choice. Suddenly I said, "Wait a minute! I'm *not* a dog; I'm a daughter. I'm *not* an outsider; I'm an heir. I'm *not* a beggar; I'm a believer. I belong at the table! That seat is *mine*! Satan, you wretched thief and liar, get out of my seat!" No longer settling for crumbs, I took my place where I belonged—in the heavenly realms with "every spiritual blessing in Christ" (Eph. 1:3).

By His grace, Christ calls us to "reign in life" (Rom. 5:17). As heirs, He wants us to receive His kingdom authority. Don't sit under the table, that sorry wasteland of unbelief and defeat. No one ever reigns from there or defeats the enemy from there. If you want to pray effectively and powerfully influence your world for Christ, then you need to sit at the table with your Master, in the seat He has reserved for you. Let me say it again: Unlike the Syrophoenician woman, you must not see yourself as an outsider fighting for crumbs. It is time to see yourself as Christ sees you; it is time to rise and take your place at His banqueting table!

You prepare a table before me in the presence of my enemies. You anoint
my head with oil; my cup overflows. Surely goodness and love will
follow me all the days of my life, and I will dwell in the house of the
˙ LORD forever.

PSALM 23:5-6

What We Should Believe About Prayer

Even when we see ourselves seated with Christ at His table, it can
often seem that He is not hearing our prayers. When my son was little, one time Clay was sitting at a dinner table absorbed in conversation with other adults. Billy sat beside him, tugging on his arm.
"Daddy, Daddy," he kept pleading. Clay didn't seem to notice.
Finally Billy got up, grabbed Clay's face in his hands, and jerked it
toward him. "Daddy!" he said emphatically. Well, he got his dad's
attention!

Sometimes that is how it seems at God's table, too. We pray, but
the Lord does not seem to be listening. We wonder if He is either
uninterested or disgusted with us or our petition. We wonder where
we went wrong and cry, "Turn your ear to me!" (Ps. 31:2; 71:2; 88:2;
102:2). But the fact that God does not immediately answer our
prayers does not mean that He has not heard and accepted them. As
with the Syrophoenician woman, the Lord has His reasons.

So what are we to do when God seems to turn a deaf ear? We
need to listen to what God is saying. Perhaps He will tell us to sit back
and trust Him. But sometimes, equating it with humility, we wrongly
assume that the most godly attitude is one of acquiescence. We wonder how the Lord can favor someone like the Syrophoenician woman
who is so forceful, so boldly tenacious. The disciples thought her a
bullheaded nuisance; the Lord nonchalantly snubbed her. Yet despite
His seeming reluctance to bless her and despite His disciples' contempt for her, she would not be turned away. To His rebuff, she
retorted, "Yes, Lord, but . . ."

Haven't we been taught, however, to mind our manners, be

polite, and never argue with the Lord? Doesn't it seem presumptuous to say, "Yes, Lord, but . . ."? How strange that this is exactly what the Lord looked for in the woman. We forget that Jesus cannot endure Christianity with no passion. It was about the tepid faith of the Laodicean church that He warned, "I am about to spit you out of my mouth" (Rev. 3:16).

The Greek word *hupomone*—translated "patience, endurance, constancy, or perseverance"—characterizes those who do not swerve from their purpose or faith despite the greatest of trials. It may be endurance under trials: "Be . . . *patient* in affliction" (Rom. 12:12); "Blessed is the man who *perseveres* under trial" (James 1:12). Or it may be persistence or perseverance in well doing: ". . . by *persevering* produce a crop" (Luke 8:15); ". . . let us run with *perseverance* the race marked out for us" (Heb. 12:1). The question is, which kind of *hupomone* does the Lord expect from us in a given situation? We can be sure it does not mean passivity, on the one hand, or defiance, on the other.

We should always yield our hearts and lives to the Lord, and we should never fight the Lord's will. But how often do we think our circumstances are the Lord's will when they are not? How often does the devil beat on us or those we care about, and we acquiesce, saying, "Thy will be done"?

It is not God's will that your child walks away from Him, that your husband be addicted to Internet pornography, that your local schools promote immorality, that your nation sinks into ever-deepening sin, rebellion, and ultimate destruction. We, like the Syrophoenician woman, must obtain a God-given vision and hold onto it until He says, "Let go; you have done your duty." Too often we simply give up with a sanctimonious, "It's in Your hands, Lord." We must not give in to weak resignation when the Lord is trying to build in us a fighting spirit and a tenacious heart.

The Syrophoenician woman had embers in her heart that Christ fanned into flames. First ignoring her and then implying she was a "dog," He made her grow all the more tenacious in her supplication. The very thing that might cause many of us to go whimpering away, Christ can use to strengthen our resolve. When He seems to turn a deaf ear, perhaps He is drawing us to contend even more for something. When He proves our faith, He *improves* our faith. From outward appearances, our boldness may appear to displease Him. But He can treat us this way precisely because He *is* pleased with us. Behind His seeming frown of rejection is really a smile of delight. "Yes, Lord, but . . . ," she contended. She fought for "crumbs," but in the end she received the key to God's vast storehouse. And so can we.

The Lord prizes a tenacious heart. Repeatedly we see the value of tenacity in Scripture. Not only do we find people with a God-given vision who prevailed simply because they refused to take no for an answer, but the Lord praised this attitude. It amazed me to learn that the subjects of Jesus' only two parables about prayer both had tenacious hearts. Just look:

The Friend at Midnight (Luke 11:5-8)

> *Then he said to them, "Suppose one of you has a friend, and he goes to him at midnight and says, 'Friend, lend me three loaves of bread, because a friend of mine on a journey has come to me, and I have nothing to set before him.'*
>
> *"Then the one inside answers, 'Don't bother me. The door is already locked, and my children are with me in bed. I can't get up and give you anything.' I tell you, though he will not get up and give him the bread because he is his friend, yet because of the man's boldness he will get up and give him as much as he needs."*

Here is a man with a tenacious heart who will not take no for an answer. Unwilling to settle for crumbs, he wants every loaf in the house! He is presumptuous. Yet Christ commends him as an example of how we should pray, and He sums up the main point of the parable with these famous words: "So I say to you: Ask and it will be given to you; seek and you will find; knock and the door will be opened to you. For everyone who asks receives; he who seeks finds; and to him who knocks, the door will be opened" (Luke 11:9-10).

In the context, we see that God honors the one who tenaciously asks, seeks, and knocks. I think of how often I have politely knocked or even resorted to banging once or twice. When the Lord didn't answer, however, I went away withdrawn, dejected, confused, and defeated. But what is He saying in this parable? "Don't give up!" Have stick-to-itiveness and fervency in your prayer-life. Keep asking, seeking, and knocking with a tenacious heart until you see Him answer. If you are convinced of His will, and something just does not seem to be happening, keep pounding fervently on the door until it comes.

The Unjust Judge (Luke 18:1-8)

Then Jesus told his disciples a parable to show them that they should always pray and not give up. He said: "In a certain town there was a judge who neither feared God nor cared about men. And there was a widow in that town who kept coming to him with the plea, 'Grant me justice against my adversary.'

"For some time he refused. But finally he said to himself, 'Even though I don't fear God or care about men, yet because this widow keeps bothering me, I will see that she gets justice, so that she won't eventually wear me out with her coming!'"

And the Lord said, "Listen to what the unjust judge says. And will not God bring about justice for his chosen ones, who cry out to him day and night? Will he keep putting them off? I tell you, he will see that they get justice, and quickly. However, when the Son of Man comes, will he find faith on the earth?"

Again Jesus teaches us to pray and not give up. He tells of a woman with a tenacious heart whose pressing need drives her to persist until she gets what she wants. Quite possibly His encounter with the Syrophoenician woman inspired this teaching.

The Scriptures tell of many people, like the Syrophoenician woman, who had tenacious hearts when it came to receiving God's blessing. Blind Bartimaeus heard Jesus passing by and shouted, "Jesus, Son of David, have mercy on me!" Evidently he disgusted lots of people because "many rebuked him and told him to be quiet." How did he respond? "He shouted all the more." So Jesus stopped everything and healed him (Mark 10:46-52).

I also think of Jacob out in the wilderness wrestling with God all night until he got his blessing. He vowed, "I will not let you go unless you bless me." It was a long night for Jacob, and he might have even grown discouraged. But he wrestled on until he heard the Lord say, "Your name will no longer be Jacob, but Israel, because you have struggled with God and with men and have overcome." It was almost as if the Lord told him, "You have conquered. Here, the blessing is yours!" (Gen. 32:24-30). When we tenaciously press in and "wrestle" God for our blessing despite distressing hurdles, disillusioning obstacles, and depressing setbacks, that is prevailing prayer.

Like the little woman from Tyre, will you keep coming back to God in faith? Will you refuse to let go? Without her crisis, she might never have felt a need for Jesus, let alone prevailed in her intercession. But her trouble brought her to Jesus' feet. Everything pointed against it, but she knew He had a blessing for her. She had no ethnic or religious claim at all on Jesus, and some might consider her request illegitimate. But she would not let herself be shut out. Tenaciously contending for Christ's blessing, she received it.

Dear sister in Christ, you *do* have a legitimate claim on Him. If you trust in His atoning work on the cross for you, you are His child. That means you have a position at His table to claim; you have rights to enjoy. Will you do it? What is it that you want from the Lord? What do you care about enough that you would not take no for an answer? Have you a desperate need or a passionate vision? Has God given you a golden promise or a prophetic word to claim? Do not let yours be the kind of faith that timidly asks once and goes away. Do not let yours be the kind that asks boldly once and goes away. Let yours be the kind that asks boldly once and then again . . . and again . . . for as long as it takes.

Will you renew your belief in your God-given vision? Will you in faith latch onto the God-given result? With a tenacious heart will you press in until you see it accomplished? God's promises are incalculably precious and vast, the Holy Spirit's resources inestimably powerful and abundant. So with empowered determination, shake off a haphazard, half-hearted, lackluster faith. Be done with crumbs! Have unrelenting confidence in our Lord's promises and lay claim to the incredible rights and privileges you have as His offspring.

Let us wrestle from the devil's clutches our families, our cities, our nation, and our world. Let's bring them to Christ, to wholeness, to victory through our prayers and *shatter* the power of darkness. When we come like the Syrophoenician woman did that day—even putting up with abuse, pain, and rejection, persisting in prayer against Satan's strongholds—we will prevail with joy. She was a conqueror, and *we* have the promise that through Christ we are *more* than conquerors.

For Zion's sake I will not keep silent, for Jerusalem's sake I will not remain quiet, till her righteousness shines out like the dawn, her salvation like a blazing torch.

ISAIAH 62:1

Never be lacking in zeal, but keep your spiritual fervor, serving the Lord.

ROMANS 12:11

Heart Check

1. Can you think of a time when you wrestled in prayer until God answered you?

2. As you examine your heart, do you see hindrances that keep you

from having a bolder, more tenacious heart for the things you believe in?

3. What can you do to overcome those things?

4. What is the most important principle you can apply to your life from the Syrophoenician woman's example?

5. Compose a prayer to God in response to this chapter's truths.

3

The Queen of Sheba

THE SEARCHING HEART

1 KINGS 10:1-13; 2 CHRONICLES 9:1-12; MATTHEW 12:42; LUKE 11:31

"SOLOMON, SOLOMON, SOLOMON. All I hear is Solomon this and Solomon that! Haven't I heard enough? You may go!" The official fled from his queen's presence, leaving her alone in her courtroom with her thoughts. She had tried hard to maintain her composure, but all the world was abuzz with rumors of Israel's king. She felt frustrated. Truth be told though, she was as curious about Solomon as anyone.

Although the queen was not yet ready to reveal her intense interest, the fantastic accounts made her heart burn with wonder. Rumor had it that none other than the God of gods had endowed this Israeli king with his stupendous wisdom, and no problem was too difficult for him. He could supposedly solve every puzzle, understand every riddle, and give insight into every kind of dilemma. He could not be stymied.

Perplexed and brimming with questions, the queen wondered, *How much of what I am hearing is fact and how much fiction? How can any mortal be so wise?* She stood up and began to pace the room. *Who is this King Solomon anyway? How did he get his wisdom? From his God? How can I learn more about this God? If only I knew the truth.*

Clearly agitated, she plopped herself down again. *Humph! What is this strange religion? How can one god be the only true and living God, the ultimate source of all wisdom, as Israel claims? How can a single deity really have infinite wisdom? What about the collective wisdom of my own gods—sun, moon, and star gods? What am I to think?* She stood up again. *Maybe I'm just getting carried away with second-hand exaggerated reports. Then again . . . what if it's all true?* Walking over to a window, she peered out in Israel's direction. *How can I learn more about Solomon . . . and his God?* The queen could not push her questions aside. She wanted to know; she longed to know; she *had* to know the answers.

Outwardly she had it all—beauty, wealth, and power. But her best asset, a heart hungry for wisdom, would spur her to search without reserve for the truth until she found it. It mattered not the expense or the distance or even the sacrifice. That is why we call the Queen of Sheba's heart The Searching Heart.

Who was this queen, and what do we know about her? Though she is unnamed in Scripture, she has been assigned various names in Eastern legends. Her name is Makeda in Ethiopian legends; Arabs call her Bilkis. Her country, Sheba (the Hebrew spelling of Saba), was a great and wealthy trading community of southwestern Arabia during the first millennium B.C. She ruled from about 950 to 930 B.C., the same time King Solomon ruled Jerusalem. We note with interest that Sabaean women could occupy such high positions. Both Assyrian and southern Arabian inscriptions testify to the existence of queens in early pre-Islamic Arabia.

The Sabaean civilization was renowned for its control over trade in many products from Africa, India, and the East. Dominating overland trade routes, Sabaeans traded in gold, frankincense, sweet cane, spices, gems, and other goods. Ezekiel 27:22 speaks of the merchants of Sheba who traded the finest of all kinds of spices, precious stones, and gold. Solomon in Psalm 72:15 said, "Long may he (the king) live! May gold from Sheba be given to him."

Sabaeans were originally nomads, but probably by Solomon's time they had settled in the eastern area of what is roughly modern Yemen. Modern archaeologists have discovered that in southwest

Arabia a highly developed Sabaean kingdom existed in Solomon's time. Excavations of Ma'rib, the capital, have revealed a great dam reflecting highly developed engineering skills. More significantly, excavations are currently underway to learn more about the Temple of the Moon God (the Mahram Bilqis). A Canadian professor heading up a three-year project claims that this imposing temple is much larger than archaeologists had previously anticipated, perhaps the size of the entire University of Calgary campus (526 acres). Since so many the world over find the Queen of Sheba fascinating—she is found both in the Bible and Koran—these ancient ruins promise to become a major cultural and tourist draw for Yemen.

Despite the size of her temples and the wealth of her kingdom, the Queen of Sheba felt a longing in her heart for something that her gods could not offer and her wealth could not buy. She possessed so much in her own country. Why would she go searching far off for more? Wouldn't it seem logical that a queen would send emissaries for her? Ordinarily, yes, but Solomon with his mind-boggling wisdom had captured her imagination. She felt she must go. She must find that higher knowledge that came from Israel's God—"the wisdom of Solomon" (Luke 11:31 NRSV).

To understand Solomon's wisdom that so stunned the world and captivated the queen, we must look at how God had worked in his life. As the new king and heir to his famous father, David, young Solomon felt overwhelmed. David had known how to run a kingdom, but he was dead and gone. Solomon needed help—*God's* help—and He knew it. One day he traveled five miles from Jerusalem to the city of Gibeon, the site of the tabernacle, to seek the Lord and offer sacrifices. God took special notice as the new king offered a thousand burnt offerings.

That night the Lord came to Solomon in a dream. No typical dream, this was an extraordinary divine visitation. The Lord said to him, "Ask for whatever you want me to give you" (1 Kings 3:5). Solomon already felt overwhelmed with the task of ruling the vast and challenging nation. He replied that he felt like a little child next to his overwhelming responsibility. "So give your servant a discerning heart," he said, "to govern your people and to distinguish between right and wrong. For who is able to govern this great people of yours?" (1 Kings 3:9).

It pleased the Lord that Solomon had not asked for his own personal benefit but for the good of the people he governed. It pleased Him so greatly, in fact, that He promised Solomon "a wise and discerning heart, so that there will never have been anyone like you, nor will there ever be" (1 Kings 3:12). Not only that, God also promised something Solomon had not asked for—such riches and honor that in his lifetime no other king would rival him. (Note: This story is found in 1 Kings 3:4-15.)

The Lord wasted no time in fulfilling His promises. Solomon quickly emerged as a king vastly superior in wealth and wisdom to all other kings of the earth. His fame spread throughout Arabia among people famous for their wisdom. Soon the whole world had heard of him, and it seemed all the earth sought an audience with him to hear the incredible wisdom God had poured into his mind and heart (1 Kings 10:23-24).

Finally the Queen of Sheba had heard enough. Her curiosity and fascination produced such a restless burning in her heart that she simply had to go and meet this so-called "wisest and wealthiest of kings." She would judge the claims for herself.

Contests involving riddles or proverbs were popular in the East for testing practical wisdom. Arabs loved matching wits in this way. The queen was no exception. She likely called on her gods and summoned her kingdom's wisest minds as she set to work at finding the most mysterious and challenging questions possible to pose to Solomon. With the help of her advisers, she formulated the very best ones for her anticipated royal appointment.

The queen had little interest in playing games, however. She was on a serious quest for truth and was prepared to test its authenticity.

If Israel's king could answer her tough riddles, it would mean that Israel really did have an incredibly wise God who had endowed His servant with divine wisdom. If Solomon could prevail, then she would be forced to believe in the supremacy of this God over any god she worshiped. She would have to admit that she had encountered a matchless truth.

Her journey to Israel would be no joy ride. She would travel across the desert for some twelve hundred hot and tedious miles. There would be hazards, and the trip would take the queen away from the domestic affairs of her kingdom for what might be a dangerously long period. Nevertheless, this search could bring enormous rewards, not just to her, but to her kingdom. She could justify her costly expedition to Israel by pointing to the possibility of negotiating a trade agreement with the wealthy Israeli king. This, no doubt, would have been in the best interests of the Sabaean economy.

So the queen set out for Jerusalem hoping to pit her wisdom and wealth against Solomon's. Along with her tough questions, she carried with her an enormous sampling of her own wealth. Crossing the Arabian desert with her caravan weighted down with gifts and provisions was no easy feat. Travel by camel was the best transportation of the day. Still, it was not the most pleasant way for a queen to travel— smelly animals, scorching heat, endless desert, swirling sands, and taunting mirages day after day. Yet the Queen of Sheba did not turn back. Her heart was on a search of utmost importance to her.

My heart says of you, "Seek his face!" Your face, LORD, I will seek.
PSALM 27:8

When the caravan finally crested the last desert hill, there stretched before their eyes was a most breathtaking city—Jerusalem! The weary travelers spruced themselves up and tried to look as fresh and regal as they could. As they entered this foreign culture, they must have wondered greatly. Signs of prosperity greeted them everywhere. They marveled as they passed by the magnificent temple to a deity yet unknown to them.

Years before at the temple's dedication, Solomon had prayed prophetically, "Likewise when a foreigner, who is not of your people Israel, comes from a distant land because of your name—for they shall hear of your great name, your mighty hand, and your outstretched arm—when a foreigner comes and prays toward this house, then hear in heaven your dwelling place, and do according to all that the foreigner calls to you, so that all the peoples of the earth may know your name and fear you, as do your people Israel, and so that they may know that your name has been invoked on this house that I have built" (1 Kings 8:41-43 NRSV). What a prayer! Since God's ultimate intention for the nation of Israel was for it to be a beacon to the world, this was the type of prayer God loved to answer. And so He had.

The caravan of the Queen of Sheba was likely the most imposing one ever to enter Jerusalem. Large crowds must have gathered rapidly as rumor spread that an Arabian queen from a faraway land had come to see King Solomon. They gawked in stunned silence as camel after camel carrying ornately decorated chests passed by. It was "a very great caravan—with camels carrying spices, large quantities of gold, and precious stones" (1 Kings 10:2). Finally the procession came to rest before the glittering splendor of Solomon's palace.

The queen and her entourage received a royal welcome. They were provided everything they needed for their refreshment. Nevertheless, the queen likely could think of little else but what she had come for—an audience with the famed king of Israel. Brimming over with the best of questions—skillfully crafted and difficult to answer—she probably had rehearsed her interview repeatedly during her journey.

When the time for her private sitting with the king finally arrived, she entered his throne room with an impressive display of her own regalia. But when she saw Solomon's splendor, she grew weak. There he sat in splendid attire on his massive throne made of fine gold inlaid with ivory. Two large sculptured lions stood at either side of the throne. Six wide steps led up to the throne with lions at the ends of each step. With a total of fourteen lions, "nothing like it had ever been made for any other kingdom" (1 Kings 10:20).

After their introductions, she carefully began to pose her varied questions, first one, then another. Solomon was pleased to listen to them all. Though they were of a very great difficulty, he quickly and graciously gave a fitting response to each one. None were too deep, too complex, too perplexing. To her amazement, he consistently had the perfect solution to every riddle, question, and puzzle.

As those who later tested Christ's wisdom were awestruck and humbled and left unable to test Him further (Matt. 22:46), the queen ran out of courage to go on. To say that Solomon's wisdom *astounded* her would be an understatement. His wisdom far exceeded all accounts. *Where could such infinite wisdom come from,* she wondered, *if not from the God whom King Solomon acknowledges?*

As she toured the palace Solomon had built, its magnificence deeply impressed her. The elegance of his table, the superb cuisine, the exquisite goblets and other articles all made of pure gold, the dignified seating of his officials, the lavish attire of even his servants and cupbearers, the efficient management of his affairs—everything amazed her! In fact, all she had witnessed—the city, the buildings, the projects, the palace—utterly fascinated her.

Filled with admiration, the queen asked Solomon many questions concerning his God and temple worship. She had not known this holy, sovereign, invisible God who exacts punishment on sin and yet mercifully provides atonement. Escorted to the temple, she noted its glorious appearance and its careful management by the priests and Levites. She watched the king as he proceeded majestically up the temple steps to humble himself and worship his God. She wondered at his offering of a burnt sacrifice for the forgiveness of his sins.

She could tell that all the grandeur she had witnessed was somehow centered here. It was all an outward manifestation of a king who revered his God and of a God who had graciously bestowed extraordinary divine blessing and favor upon a king and his nation.

The whole revelation hit the queen hard: "there was no more spirit in her" (1 Kings 10:5 NRSV). The Hebrew word for "spirit" used here carries with it the idea of power. As a psychological term, it suggests that she had been unable to find any way to prevail in her sessions with Solomon. The weight of her experience exhausted her resources. Breathless, astounded, and overwhelmed, stripped of energy and determination, her fight was over. She succumbed to Solomon's wisdom, accepting everything he had told her about life, eternal mysteries, temporal questions, practical matters, and a host of other things. Her visit had convinced her.

Unable to contain her awe and wonder, she humbly declared, "The report I heard in my own country about your achievements and your wisdom is true. But I did not believe these things until I came and saw with my own eyes. Indeed, not even half was told me; in wisdom and wealth you have far exceeded the report I heard. How happy your men must be! How happy your officials, who continually stand before you and hear your wisdom!" Then she exulted, "Praise be to the LORD your God, who has delighted in you and placed you on the throne of Israel. Because of the LORD's eternal love for Israel, he has made you king, to maintain justice and righteousness"(1 Kings 10:6-9).

The Queen of Sheba may have come to Jerusalem thinking to find some kind of worldly wisdom. Instead she found the Source of all wisdom. Jewish writers believe that this pagan queen was converted at this time to the worship of the true God. Her search was over. She had found her treasure; she had found the truth.

The queen waited until the end of her visit to give her rich gifts to King Solomon. Her heart now full, she joyously presented them as tokens of her appreciation—great quantities of rare spices, large amounts of precious stones, 120 talents of gold ($5 million or more).

Yet the queen could not outgive Solomon. Responding with his own grandiose display of liberality, he lavished rich gifts from his own bounty upon her. He then went on to offer her whatever else she might want. What he gave her by far exceeded in generosity what she had given him. But how could a monetary value be placed upon the rich spiritual treasure she had received?

The Queen of Sheba's famous visit was a well-known story to the Jews of Jesus' generation. Jesus contrasted her willingness to make the arduous journey with the Jews' complacency. He lambasted the religious hypocrites of His day by pointing to her example, exposing their pride and prejudice in contrast to the humble openness and searching of this Gentile queen. He said, "The Queen of the South will rise at the judgment with this generation and condemn it; because she came from the ends of the earth to listen to Solomon's wisdom, and now one greater than Solomon is here" (Matt. 12:42; Luke 11:31).

The someone greater, of course, was Jesus Christ Himself. Though He was right there with the Jews, they refused to accept Him. While they probed and scrutinized the Lord, appearing to search for the truth, they didn't really want it. If their hearts had been honest in their search, wouldn't they have gladly acknowledged the truth? Wouldn't they have immediately fallen down before their long-awaited Messiah in worship?

The Queen of Sheba presents a contrasting picture—willing to pay any price to search out the truth for herself. She came seeking wisdom, ready to put Solomon to the test to see if his was a truly divinely inspired wisdom. Jesus noted that she had spared no cost or convenience in seeking God's wisdom.

While the Jews deprived themselves, this foreign queen found rich treasure—more than she could have imagined. How can we know that this woman with a searching heart had genuinely found this treasure? Because Jesus says that while hypocrites fall, she will stand in the judgment.

Little did the Queen of Sheba know that her search for truth would ultimately lead her to bow at the feet of the one true and living God. Nor did she have any idea that her trip would stand in history's annals as one of the most famous pilgrimages of all time. The kings of the earth had sought the privilege of an audience with King Solomon, but the Scriptures do not mention them. The queen is the only one besides David's friend Hiram whose visit the Scripture specifically documents. It seems certain that in Solomon's mind the most significant visit by a foreign dignitary must have been this one by the Sabaean queen.

It was Solomon who had personified wisdom, saying, "Prize her highly, and she will exalt you; she will honor you if you embrace her. She will place on your head a fair garland; she will bestow on you a beautiful crown" (Prov. 4:8-9 NRSV). Though the Queen of Sheba had embarked on her search wearing one crown, she went home wearing a more significant one—the crown of wisdom. Not only that, but now her heart brimmed over with rich and wondrous spiritual treasure. Truly, her search for wisdom ended in a resounding triumph over the ignorance that had so long bound her heart and life.

In proclaiming the future glory of Zion, Isaiah prophesied a specific promise to the descendants of the Queen of Sheba: "And all from Sheba will come, bearing gold and incense and proclaiming the praise of the LORD" (Isa. 60:6). The influence of her powerful conversion experience would live on.

My child, if you accept my words and treasure up my commandments within you, making your ear attentive to wisdom and inclining your heart to understanding; if you indeed cry out for insight, and raise your voice for understanding; if you seek it like silver, and search for it as for hidden treasures—then you will understand the fear of the LORD and find the knowledge of God.

PROVERBS 2:1-5 NRSV (EMPHASIS MINE)

LESSONS FOR OUR OWN HEARTS

Although she possessed vast earthly wealth, the Queen of Sheba sensed a need in her life. She felt her heart stir as so many do, but she, unlike many others, refused to stop there. Merely desiring the truth was not enough for her. She made the deliberate choice to do something about it—something radical that might cost her everything as she left her home to travel to the ends of the earth. Unaware that the God of all truth was inspiring her spiritual hunger, she set out on a spiritual quest that would lead her straight to the only-wise God, the ultimate Source of all truth.

Perhaps you feel that you have already found God. You think you have no reason for searching any further. But do you really know Him? Into how much of His life and into what depth of His treasures have you really tapped? Whatever your answer, you can be assured that He has more for you. All of us need to awaken to the adventure of seeking Him and His kingdom as a way of life. We can never fully comprehend our awesome God, but He does want to take us to greater heights of revelation and depths of relationship than we have yet understood or experienced.

Do you wistfully long for more out of life? Are you bored with your Christian walk? Do you wonder if God has more for you in terms of your love relationship with Him? Do you desire a fresh fire, fresh infilling, fresh anointing? Then go for it! I believe that if we continually search to know God and His purposes more fully, our faith will never be boring or humdrum. On the contrary, life will be a perpetual adventure. We will enjoy His mysteries revealed and His mercies made new *every* morning.

My first life-changing "Daniel fast" ushered me into a whole new and wonderful phase of relating with God. (I wrote about this experience in *Healing for the Heart*, pp. 176-178.) Since then I have made it my practice to seek God each year during the first twenty-one days of January. Like Daniel, I refrain from meat and delicacies during those twenty-one days and try to seek God more diligently than usual. For me, it seems meant to be. I always break my fast on January 22, my birthday, with yummy birthday indulgences.

Is it time for you to renew or even begin an active pursuit of God? Then earnestly pray and ask God to direct you. He wants you to desire earnestly to know Him better. He wants you to seek Him above all other things. He has revelations to give you, truths for you to unwrap, joys in His presence.

The poor and needy search for water, but there is none; their tongues are parched with thirst. But I the LORD will answer them; I, the God of Israel, will not forsake them. I will make rivers flow on barren heights, and springs within the valleys. I will turn the desert into pools of water, and the parched ground into springs.

ISAIAH 41:17-18

He rewards those who earnestly seek him.

HEBREWS 11:6

Conducting a successful spiritual search requires a number of things. Let's look at a few of them.

Passion for Truth

The Queen of Sheba possessed a "holy discontent"; she was dissatisfied with things as they were. The longing in her heart motivated her to go the distance—some twelve hundred grueling miles across the parched Arabian desert—in search of truth. Many people puzzle over spiritual issues; they have a great many questions. Yet when it comes to taking any real action to find answers, they complacently shrug their shoulders. Letting the issue pass is so much easier.

Many in Jesus' day followed Him enthusiastically for a while. But they were interested primarily in miracles and thrills and had little interest in really knowing Him. He had not captivated their hearts. When things got tough, the crowds thinned out in a hurry.

The book of Acts, on the other hand, cites the Berean Christians as a good example of what Christ looks for in those who claim to want God. Scripture attests that they were "more noble" than the Thessalonians. Why? Because, like the Queen of Sheba, their fervent hearts drove them to know the truth. Having picked up the scent, hot on the trail, they searched the Scriptures daily to see whether the Gospel being preached to them was really true (Acts 17:10-11). Once they knew the truth, they became so devoted that they refused to betray it.

How about you? Are you an inquiring soul, eager for knowledge, inclined to investigate the Gospel's claims earnestly? When people greet you with hard questions, are you ready with wise answers because you have already gone the distance to find the answers for yourself?

There is a lot of passivity and complacency in the church today. It seems that some of us think that trusting God implies sitting on the pew and doing nothing spiritually. But God wants us to conduct an earnest and honest search for fuller revelations of His nature, will, and purpose for our lives and for our world.

Perhaps you have been content to let others spoon-feed you. Those who allow this as a way of life will suffer from stunted spiritual growth and end up just "fat little babies." Letting others do their thinking for them, these people will be particularly vulnerable to deception. I have seen this happen to Christian brothers and sisters I know personally, with tragic results. If you are looking for someone to tell you how to think and what to do, there's bound to be someone out there happy to oblige you. But Jesus charges you, "Seek and *you* will find" (Matt. 7:7). That is, *you* seek God—His face, His favor, His way, His truth, and His life with *your* whole heart, and He promises to give everything else to you.

It frightens me—no, terrifies me!—that so many of God's people are so willing to believe a charismatic leader simply because of his eloquence. This person may be spewing out doctrinal heresy or living immorally, seeking money, sex, and power. But because the person is confident, assertive, and attractive, somehow he or she is beyond scrutiny. "Touch not the Lord's anointed" is their deceptive shield. Unfortunately, anyone who questions this leader's biblical or moral faithfulness is often seen as a troublemaker or alarmist.

True, there are those who assault leaders out of rebellion against authority or because of excessive concern for theological minutiae, and we need to watch out for them. But it is also vitally important that, in our love for Christ and His truth, we hold our leaders accountable to the truth of the Gospel and to the lifestyle espoused in God's Word. Do you have a passion for God's truth?

Dear friends, do not believe every spirit, but test the spirits to see whether they are from God, because many false prophets have gone out into the world.

1 JOHN 4:1

Test everything. Hold on to the good.

1 THESSALONIANS 5:21

In these end times we should *all* be diligent when it comes to the truth. We live in an age increasingly influenced by Eastern philosophies that try to convince us to stop thinking and just "be." Absolutes are rapidly disintegrating around us. Many in the church boast that they don't care about doctrine. But when we place personas or experiences above doctrinal truth, we are in grave danger. Paul, a passionate champion for the truth, charges us, "Do your best to present yourself to God as one approved, a workman who does not need to be ashamed and who correctly handles the word of truth" (2 Tim. 2:15). The Greek word translated here "do your best"—*spoudazo*—indicates a speedy, earnest, diligent, and careful pursuit of truth. The Lord approves of those who wisely and responsibly handle God's truth.

Why should we obey Paul's admonition? He goes on to explain that the teachings of those who wander from the truth will be like gangrene that spreads to destroy true faith (2 Tim. 2:17-18). He then warns of the last days when people will always be "learning but never able to acknowledge the truth" (2 Tim. 3:7) and when "wicked people and impostors will go from bad to worse, deceiving others and being deceived" (2 Tim. 3:13 NRSV).

Jesus Christ charges believers, "If you hold to my teaching, you are really my disciples. Then you will know the truth, and the truth will set you free" (John 8:31-32). Not only will the truth set us free, but by preserving legitimate faith in Christ, it will keep us free.

Are you ready to ask the Lord for a passionately hungry heart for His truth? You can find tremendous blessing if you seek wisdom as did Solomon, the Queen of Sheba, and the Bereans. You can also be a powerful witness to others who need to know the truth.

Humility

Even though she was already a reigning monarch, the Queen of Sheba possessed an incredible measure of humility. It took humility to realize her own limitations and admit, "I know I don't know it all; I know there is more, and I am willing to humble myself before King Solomon, his God, and all the world if that's what it takes." It took humility to admit and accept the truth when she found it.

In stark contrast, many in Jesus' time had neither desire nor tolerance for anything more from God. Most of the religious leaders feigned interest in the truth. They studied Scripture religiously; they asked Jesus hard questions. But their hearts were dishonest; they had "rejected God's purpose for themselves" (Luke 7:30). Condemning their sham search for truth, Jesus lambasted them: "You diligently study the Scriptures because you think that by them you possess eternal life. These are the Scriptures that testify about me, yet you refuse to come to me to have life" (John 5:39-40). Why did they not sincerely seek wisdom? Because they knew they would not like what they found. The truth would offend their sense of personal righteousness. It would call them to bow their stubborn hearts to God's will.

Similarly, many today seem hungry for truth. Searching here and there, they read books, take in lectures, visit "sacred" sites. They appear to have open minds and hearts. Do they though? Clay and I once struck up a conversation with a politically correct university student sitting across from us on a bus. I noticed her book bag covered with buttons shouting her concern for overcoming ignorance and intolerance, her passion for truth, her quest for solutions to the world's problems. One of her buttons really grabbed my attention: "It's a beautiful thing to lose a closed mind."

As we talked with the young woman, we tried to share the Lord with her. In a short time, I grew weary, but Clay tried to reason with her about the Lord for a good hour or two. Finally he challenged her: "If Jesus Christ came to you in a way that absolutely convinced you that He is who He said He was, the divine Son of God, would you submit to Him?"

She said, "Absolutely not! I would *never* submit to Jesus Christ."

So much for her open-minded desire for truth. So many who pretend to be open to truth simply do not have the humility or willingness to submit to the truth when they find it. They commend each other for openness to truth even though they are not open at all. They sift through their smorgasbord of "truths" to find what most pleases their egos or their senses—whatever enables them to make their own rules, live as they want to live, and be their own gods.

In his pride the wicked does not seek him; in all his thoughts there is no room for God.

PSALM 10:4

Are you humble enough to recognize your inadequacy, to cast off all smug self-righteousness? If not, any spiritual search you undertake will lead nowhere except back to your own fallen self. A genuine spiritual journey requires a humble willingness to conform to the truth when you find it. The poor in spirit, the humble—these are the ones whose search ends in triumph. They discover the wondrous riches of God's kingdom.

Courage and Diligence

Did a panel of naysayers in Sheba object to their queen's intentions to leave on a pilgrimage? No doubt. She understood the arguments. Her entire kingdom would have to wait as she sought the wisdom of another kingdom. Besides the valuable months away from important affairs of state, such an expedition would take great effort and expense. How could she, a pampered and exalted queen, realistically trade the comforts of her palace for a long, uncomfortably hot and dangerous journey—for who knows what? It would take courageous sacrifice and a willingness to jeopardize herself politically. Yet once the queen made her decision, she would not be deterred.

What price will you pay? Would you, like the Queen of Sheba, courageously decide that no effort is too great and no price to high for the Lord? Would you courageously venture out from the safety and security of your own land, people, and ways in order to investigate rumors of things God is doing in this world today? Would you venture to the next town to a conference, seminar, or Bible study? Would you go down the street to your local Christian bookstore for a good book? Would you sit in your own home and study God's Word?

Spiritually perilous times demand spiritually earnest believers. The spirit of the age increasingly boasts that truth is irrelevant, unknowable, or relative—that you can choose from a variety of beliefs and not be any worse off than anyone else. But the Bible warns that deception will grip this world.

Last year our Christian school nearly hired a certain teacher.

When Clay pinned him down theologically, he admitted that he would have a hard time telling a Buddhist or Hindu that their truth was less valid than Christ's truth. Here was a man who not only became confused about the issue of truth but who would pass his error on to our children. While he may have been a nice and well-meaning "Christian" man, he was heretical in his thinking and unqualified to teach the children of believers.

Is this some isolated incident? I think not. Heretics abound in the church today. Why? Often because the truth is not palatable to people, they reconstruct it to make it more acceptable. In our day, it takes courage to stand for unadulterated truth, to say, "I'm not a relativist. I believe in absolute truth." Jesus, calling Himself the stone that the builders rejected, predicted, "Everyone who falls on that stone will be broken to pieces, but he on whom it falls will be crushed" (Luke 20:18). The Lord didn't have the slightest interest in adapting His truth to fit our tastes.

Do you truly want to be a woman of wisdom, one who knows gospel truth? Do you want to be one who strengthens the church by refusing to compromise the truth? Then forget the "drive-through," "feed me," instant-gratification mentality so prominent today. Make it your first priority to know and understand God. Open your heart to Him anew; renounce complacency; forsake the safety of shallow security; roll up your sleeves and strike out on an exciting spiritual odyssey. The Lord is waiting to direct you to fuller revelations of His will and purpose.

In the heat of the cruel desert, the Queen of Sheba surely must at times have wondered whether her search was really worth it. When she considered what she might find—a desert mirage or an oasis for her soul—she courageously pressed on, and her heart search ended in triumph. Joyfully discovering the incredible riches of God's truth, she could testify with Solomon, "Happy are those who find wisdom, and those who get understanding, for her income is better than silver, and her revenue better than gold. She is more

precious than jewels, and nothing you desire can compare with her"
(Prov. 3:13-15 NRSV).

"For I know the plans I have for you," declares the LORD, "plans to prosper you and not to harm you, plans to give you hope and a future. Then you will call upon me and come and pray to me, and I will listen to you. You will seek me and find me when you seek me with all your heart."

JEREMIAH 29:11-13

The Sabaean queen found far more than her heart had ever intended or even imagined. She exclaimed that not even half was told her of all the wisdom and glory she witnessed. Likewise, our God has vastly more of His riches to reveal to us. Just try to capture a glimpse of what He has for you to discover. Paul prays that we might "be filled with all the fullness of God" (Eph. 3:19 NRSV). *All* the fullness of God? That means all the riches to be found in Him—the love and grace of God, the righteousness and peace of Christ, the gifts and graces of His Spirit, wisdom concerning the ways of God, knowledge concerning the will of God, insight concerning the mysteries of God, manna from heaven for our hearts, living water for our souls, eternal communion for our spirits.

Paul concludes his thought—just listen to this!—assuring us that the Lord "is able to carry out His purpose and do superabundantly, far over and above all that we dare ask or think—infinitely beyond our highest prayers, desires, thoughts, hopes or dreams" (Eph. 3:20 AMPLIFIED). Again Christ promises, "Seek and you will *find*" (Matt. 7:7). Have we even scratched the surface of what God wants us to *find* in Christ?

Will you choose to become a devoted treasure-hunter, one who searches diligently for the riches of God's kingdom? Then renounce the hindrances, work to overcome the obstacles, and launch out toward your destiny. Your search, like that of the Queen of Sheba, will prove a joyously rich and rewarding one. Amazing discoveries of wisdom, purpose, love, and joy await you.

But seek first his kingdom and his righteousness, and all these things will be given to you as well.

MATTHEW 6:33

All night long on my bed I looked for the one my heart loves; I looked for him but did not find him. I will get up now and go about the city, through its streets and squares; I will search for the one my heart loves. So I looked for him but did not find him. The watchmen found me as they made their rounds in the city. "Have you seen the one my heart loves?" Scarcely had I passed them when I found the one my heart loves. I held him and would not let him go. . . .

SONG OF SOLOMON 3:1-4

Heart Check

1. Would you best describe your spiritual life as standing still or moving forward?

2. What would you like to discover in your relationship with God?

3. What are some things you can do to prepare your heart for a profitable quest for spiritual enrichment?

4. Are you willing, once finding God's truth, to conform your lifestyle to it?

5. Compose a prayer in response to the truths in this chapter.

4

Deborah

THE VALIANT HEART

JUDGES 4—5

THERE IT IS! A feeling of relief swept over Barak. Having just come some sixty miles from the far north, Kedesh in Naphtali, he had been looking for the landmark. Now he saw it—a lone palm tree standing tall on the Ephraim hillside. There could be no doubt about it, for palm trees were rare in Palestine. More telling, however, was the tent beneath it. Its flaps were open to catch the afternoon breezes, and a line of people stood waiting to gain an audience with the one inside. *What a marvel,* he thought. *All those people waiting to see a . . . a woman.* He snorted as he neared the place, remembering that he had wasted no time responding to her call.

She saw him coming, for she had been watching for him. Standing to her feet, she addressed the crowd something to this effect: "I'm not hearing any more cases today. You can come back tomorrow." Looking again toward Barak, she corrected herself, "No, on second thought, make it next month."

As the unhappy crowd dispersed, she strode out to greet her arriving guest. He had nearly forgotten the many reasons for her legendary greatness. Now watching her approach, he swallowed hard. Her presence generated awe in him—the fire in her eyes, the bold determination in her step, the iron-core air of authority about her. In a time when very few stood tall, she was a tower like her rare palm tree.

Who was she? Deborah, the acclaimed prophetess and leader of Israel, a woman of enormous wisdom, faith, and courage.

I wonder why she called for me. Barak tried to straighten his shoulders, but he was sure she could perceive the truth. He felt weak, emasculated, and depressed. The Canaanites, bent on reclaiming the Promised Land, had beaten down the men of northern Israel to the point of despair—and their distress increased by the day. All seemed hopeless.

Barak forced a smile as Deborah greeted him. "Barak, the Lord must have blessed your journey. You got here quickly. Come inside; wash your feet; make yourself comfortable." As they sat down together, a servant brought in some barley bread, a basket of figs, and a jar of fresh water. But Deborah was not really interested in a friendly visit with the man. Matters of great urgency weighed on her heart, and she got straight to the point. She knew how things were in Barak's parts and didn't need to hear any reports about it. "Barak," she said matter-of-factly, "I summoned you here today because I have a command from the Lord Almighty for you." He again swallowed hard. She didn't have a request; God had a command. Gazing into those dark and penetrating eyes, he could find no weakness—only certainty.

Little did he know that this day Deborah would call him to do the impossible. In his wildest dreams he could not have imagined that she would commission him as General Barak and order him to assemble an army from Israel's gutless, weaponless ranks to confront their dreadful and invincible foe. But this was Deborah—a noble heroine full of faith, fortitude, and fire. Without flinching, she would not only give the command, but she would lead the charge herself, if necessary. Bravely settling for nothing less than a resounding victory for her people and glory for her God, Deborah had what we might call The Valiant Heart.

Israel, at that time, was in desperate straits from problems of its own making. The people had forsaken the Lord and chosen new gods, and the Lord had withdrawn His blessing from them, letting their pagan neighbors afflict them. This was not the first time the nation had suffered oppression for its sins. When they had entered the Promised Land (Canaan), they claimed much of the territory and subdued most of their enemies. Enjoying peace, plenty, and prosperity, they lost the will to complete their task and coexisted with the remaining Canaanites. As God had warned, these pagan strongholds corrupted the nation. So He let the king of Aram beat Israel down for eight years.

This was the era before Israel had a king, and when the people repented, the Lord raised up a judge, Othniel, to deliver them. The nation enjoyed peace for forty years under his judgeship. Following his death, though, the nation became mired in sin again. So the Lord let the Moabites oppress them another eighteen years. They repented, and He raised up another judge, Ehud, to free them. This time Israel enjoyed eighty years of peace.

But the nation forgot their former misfortunes and fell into complacency once more. They adopted the idolatrous customs of their pagan neighbors. Backslidden and filled with unbelief, they no longer thought they needed the Lord. So He withdrew His grace and let them lose their advantage. The Canaanites swept over Israel mercilessly. As a result, these were desperate times characterized by disobedience, decline, darkness, defeat, and despair. This time the Lord had let His people suffer longer and more grievously in their obstinacy and ingratitude than ever before. For twenty years He had been letting them grow wise by their misfortunes.

During this period, much of northern Israel had fallen into the hands of Jabin, a brutal Canaanite king who cruelly oppressed the nation, especially the closer tribes of Naphtali and Zebulun. Jabin maintained a standing army that beat the country into submission. The army, led by the brutal Sisera, seemed invincible. Not only did it boast a hundred thousand men, but it had nine hundred iron war chariots, the much-feared "tanks" of ancient times. Often these chariots were equipped with razors several yards in length that extended from the wheels and cut down all who stood in their path. These dreaded instruments of terror gave Sisera complete control of the plains and valleys. With the people in such a helpless state, theirs was a dispirited and fearful existence.

The countryside was a shambles. The once-unified Jewish tribes lacked cohesion and needed leadership. Danger lurked on all sides. Plundering and pillaging, marauders ravaged the land and communities. The open roads had become so hazardous that those who ventured forth had to sneak around on small winding paths. Since caravans no longer came through, trade was paralyzed. Fearing for their lives, few farmers worked their fields. Leaving their homes and wasted fields, many fled to safer parts. With travel, communication, and commerce disrupted and the people brutalized and in subjection, any patriotic spirit seemed crushed forever.

In these dark and dangerous times, God had raised Deborah up as Israel's next judge. Evidently she was married to an obscure man named Lappidoth, whom we know nothing about, except that he married her. He was not the only man that she outshone though. In a man's world, she took on the responsibilities of men, the only woman in the Bible to rise to political power by the common consent of the people. She was the only female judge among the distinguished company of judges (twelve in all) who ruled Israel between the times of Joshua and Samuel.

Deborah's prominence as a ruler is especially remarkable since the position of women in that society was distinctly subordinate. Evidently the nation suffered a leadership vacuum that enabled her to rise to power. In the face of such crying needs, no male leaders had stepped forward, so she had made herself available to God. However, while few women in history have climbed the ranks to such a place of authority and respect, she did not get there by striving, competing, or subduing men. God appointed her.

Unlike the judges of today, a biblical judge led the nation, dispensing righteousness, justice, and mercy. They administered God's laws, and they helped deliver His people from their enemies. Recognizing the anointing on Deborah's life, people came from all over the country to receive her counsel. Despite the abandoned roads everywhere, the trail that led to the Palm of Deborah, as it was called, remained well-traveled.

With her great wisdom, resolute faith, ability to hear God, strength of character, and wholehearted devotion to serving her God and country, Deborah had all the right attributes for dynamic leadership. Obviously, she was excellent at adjudicating people's problems, deciding their disputes, and solving cases they could not handle themselves. But more than mediating the controversies between them, she mediated between the people and their God. Advising and correcting them in things pertaining to God, Deborah presented His case and showed them His judgment.

Beyond her judgeship, the people recognized Deborah as a prophetess, a rare gifting in those days. In their national crisis, many wanted to find God. So they came to her with their questions, to receive her wisdom and instruction, and to hear the whole counsel of God. Deborah declared God's Word and communicated His mind and will with prophetic insight, thus rousing the people from their lethargy. With the entire nation acknowledging her as their leader, her fame spread far and wide.

The northern tribes were receiving the brunt of King Jabin's fury, but his raids may have begun to extend into southern territory. The dark clouds over the land just kept getting darker. Finally, just as before, a national consciousness developed. The people tired of trying to cope with their unbearable circumstances and came to their senses. Connecting their calamities with their sins, they repented and cried out to the Lord for mercy. He heard them.

The Lord had a solution to their troubles, and that solution sat under the palm tree. If King Jabin overlooked Deborah's influence on the nation because of her gender, he made a terrible mistake. Increasingly, as people cried to the Lord for help, they asked Deborah to pray for their deliverance. God's Spirit stirred her heart until she could no longer tolerate the plight of her people. She, too, cried to the Lord. One day she received a prophetic word from the Lord, a word that would bring an ultimate test of her mettle. It was one thing to be a prophetess and judge in a nonmilitary context, but now God would lead her into uncharted waters; her influence would extend to the battlefield. Not only would she prophesy, motivate, judge, rule, and lead—she would fight!

The Lord told Deborah to call Barak to lead a small army of ten thousand men to throw off the powerful and cruel Canaanite yoke. Her valiant heart had no trouble believing the word. It mattered not that Jabin had his huge army with nine hundred iron chariots or that Israel had none. She was confident of God's promise, certain of His presence. She had no doubt in her heart concerning the outcome. God had spoken, and that was enough for her.

Sensing the Lord's burning indignation against His people's oppressors, Deborah knew this was the time to move. She must galvanize the weak and dispirited nation into faith and action. She would stir God's people to free themselves from their wretched bondage and humiliation, starting with the man appointed as military commander.

When Barak arrived, Deborah wasted no time in telling him that Israel must attack their enemy right away. Can you imagine Barak's shock when she said words to the effect: "The Lord has had enough—and I have, too—of Israel's spinelessness before the pagans. He wants us to defeat Jabin. He has even chosen a general to lead our forces—you! I don't want you to be a mere political agitator. I don't want you to settle for anything less than God's will—the complete emancipation of our people."

God's Word says that "the wise heart will know the proper time and procedure" (Eccl. 8:5). Deborah spelled out God's strategy specifically: "The LORD, the God of Israel, commands you: 'Go, take with you ten thousand men of Naphtali and Zebulun and lead the way to Mount Tabor. I will lure Sisera, the commander of Jabin's army, with his chariots and his troops to the Kishon River and give him into your hands'" (Judg. 4:6-7).

Now the name Barak in Hebrew means "Lightning." But this lightning bolt didn't feel like it had the power to strike anything—and no wonder! After twenty years of extremely cruel oppression, he had reason to hesitate. Part of the Canaanite strategy to suppress Israel had been to confiscate all their weapons. They had no swords, spears, or shields (Judg. 5:8). If you call men to take up arms, shouldn't they have arms to take up? How do you suddenly call up an army of ten thousand ill-equipped men and say, "Come on, men, let's pick up our sticks and stones and go destroy Sisera's one hundred thousand armed and dangerous soldiers and their nine hundred iron chariots!"

Yet Deborah had just handed Barak a brilliant military strategy. Sisera's dreaded chariots could thunder through the valley, decimating it, but Barak's men would be in the highlands, safely out of their reach. This gave him small comfort though. After all, Sisera was a celebrated general—bold, experienced, fierce.

While Barak tried to make sense of it all, Deborah stood before him with unflinching resolve. She knew Sisera was no match for the Lord. The Canaanites were nothing! Sisera was defeated already! The Lord would go before Barak and lure Sisera into his hands. Barak had the Lord's unreserved promise—not "maybe I will," but "*I will* give Sisera into your hands."

We can almost hear Deborah urging cautious Barak further, "Come on, man, be valiant for God; you can do it! Now have faith, go call an army together, and get the job done! Remember—the Lord has commanded *you* to do it!"

A tribute to Deborah, Barak trusted her enough to believe the Lord's word given through her. She convinced him that this was not just her idea of what might work, but God's sure direction. She succeeded in shaking him out of his weak acquiescence to the Canaanites. Her valiant heart stirred his heart. Her words infused his heart with hope. Faith rekindled in his heart. He believed that, despite the tremendous odds against them, God was mightier than Sisera's army and would stand with him.

Nevertheless, none of this was enough to get him to go it alone. He had simply lived too long under a yoke of slavery. He could step out in faith to meet the challenge; he could confront the enemy, but he needed Deborah to go with him. She, though the weaker vessel, had the stronger faith. Not only that, but she heard from God and was God's mouthpiece. Barak wanted her to stand beside him as a sign that the Lord really was with their little army. He wanted her within earshot when the battle heated up—to advise him, encourage the troops, and pray for them all. Seeing that she was not afraid of Sisera or of his chariots, he said to her: "If you go with me, I will go; but if you don't go with me, I won't go" (Judg. 4:8). What great respect he had for Deborah and her valiant heart.

Deborah was not entirely pleased with Barak's reply, but she agreed to go. She trusted the Lord and His word to her and would not send Barak where she was unwilling to go herself. She would gladly risk her life for the freedom of her people and for the glory of God. "Very well, I will go with you," she agreed. Then, adding a prophetic word, she said, "But because of the way you are going about this, the honor will not be yours, for the LORD will hand Sisera over to a woman" (Judg. 4:9). Because Barak doubted God's ability to deliver the army into his hand without Deborah's presence, he would not have the honor of destroying the enemy's commander.

So Deborah, not wasting an extra moment, stood up to leave with Barak. The Hebrew word used here in Judges 4:9—*quwm*—means "to arise or stand up." This was a significant moment for Deborah. Later she would use the same term to describe her positive action in Judges 5:7. It took a valiant heart to refuse to sit back down under her palm tree to contemplate, speculate, and calculate. Believing firmly that God would arm them with His strength, she rose to the occasion. In holy faith and determination, the two set off together for Kedesh.

This was a time when people "did what was right in their own eyes" (Judg. 21:25 NRSV). Could the two really hope to raise an army? One reason Barak had insisted that Deborah come with him was that she could help in the recruitment. He must have feared that people, in dread of their enemy, would totally disregard his appeals. As Deborah had convinced him to cast off his unbelief for God's call, she would help him convince them to do the same.

Barak summoned the tribal chiefs of Zebulun and Naphtali to come quickly. So sure was Deborah of God's will that she acted as a conduit of faith to them. We can imagine that the leaders sent out a covert call: "The Lord has spoken through Deborah to repent of our folly, stand for the Lord, and fight off our oppressors. He has promised that our deliverance is at hand, that He will go before us to fight off the Canaanite oppressors. Now those who will join Deborah, Barak, and their Israelite brothers in battle, come meet us here in Kedesh."

Deborah commanded great respect, and men rallied from all directions, from other tribes, too, for King Jabin and Sisera were not only a threat to the northern tribes but to all of Israel. The many years of oppression, however, resulted in low numbers of recruits when compared to Joshua's army of old. But God doesn't need huge numbers to fight His battles. A small army would do—ten thousand, to be exact.

The men had come with knives, axes, scythes—whatever they had. With no horses or chariots, they were all foot soldiers. The eyes of flesh might see a sorry ragtag band of citizen-soldiers who were neither well armed nor well trained. But Deborah had eyes of faith. To her, this was the Lord's army. Her valiant heart would inspire the men to do valiantly. What they lacked in armaments, they would make up for in spirit and courage. They might not have iron chariots on their side, but God had his own chariots!

Mount Tabor, on the plain of Esdraelon about eleven miles west of the Sea of Galilee, stands at the junction of three tribal territories— Issachar, Zebulun, and Naphtali. It rises to about eighteen hundred feet, and the view from its summit is one of the most extensive and grand in Palestine. This mountain was the rallying point the Lord had chosen. The ten thousand men followed Barak up the tree-covered slopes of Mount Tabor, and Deborah went with them.

News of Barak's militia on Mount Tabor didn't take long to reach Sisera's headquarters. He quickly amassed his huge army, including his entire chariot force, and headed for the battlefield. He knew the condition of Barak's army. From all indications, there would be no contest. These rebellious Israelites would soon have to come down from the mountain into the plain. When they did, his well-honed military machine would land them a decisive blow, watering the whole valley with their blood.

But God had His plans, too. Just as He had predicted, He had lured Sisera to the place of his greatest vulnerability, not his greatest strength. Barak might have looked down, though, and worried about the vast disparity between the two armies. The plan, a frontal attack in broad daylight with no element of surprise, seemed disastrous. He might have thought it utterly ridiculous but for the fact that Deborah had sworn that God would fight for them. Could God save Israel from Sisera's ferocious army and chariots? The Jewish historian Josephus reported that the scene stretching before them so terrified Barak and his men that they would have fled had not Deborah convinced them to stay and fight.

The two armies stood facing each other—tense, alert, waiting for their signal. Suddenly a battle cry rang out. A voice reverberated over the mountain. "Go!" Deborah shouted to Israel's army. "This is the day the LORD has given Sisera into your hands. Has not the LORD gone ahead of you?" (Judg. 4:14).

Now we see the extent of Israel's complete change in morale under Deborah's inspired leadership. Hearing her prophetic declaration, their faith surged. The men, with Barak in the lead, sprang from their places, charging down the mountainside. Sisera's bloodthirsty troops must have sneered as they observed the ragtag army pathetically hustling down the slopes. But the Lord was pleased to see these victims, who had for so long cowered under cruel oppression, suddenly plunging headlong in faith down the mountain to engage Sisera's army.

The enemy, with their powerful chariots, waited confidently, but they had failed to take into account Israel's God. Right then the skies rumbled, and a torrential downpour broke out upon them. Josephus reports: "So the battle began; and when they were come to a close fight, there came down from heaven a great storm, with a vast quantity of rain and hail, and the wind blew the rain in the face of the Canaanites, and so darkened their eyes that their arrows and slings were of no advantage to them." The Israelites, on the other hand, had the storm at their backs and, realizing that it was from the Lord, took great courage.

Surely Sisera would not have been so foolish as to use his chariots in the rainy season; nor would he put his army in a strategically dangerous place. But so swift and ferocious was the freak storm that the Kishon River, normally a dry river bed, swelled quickly to become a raging torrent. Now Jabin's forces stood between Barak's army and a violent river. He could not fall back to his base camp to fight on a better day. Israel drove their enemy toward the furious river, which by now was overflowing its banks, causing Sisera's heavy chariots to bog down in the mud. Sisera's greatest strength had suddenly become his worst nightmare. Horses panicked and became uncontrollable, rearing and cutting themselves on the deadly razors. The soldiers tried to recover, but the tangled and bloody mess could not be salvaged. This threw them into a wild panic. They abandoned their mighty weapons of war and tried climbing over each other to flee for their lives. The wild and impassable river, however, swept many away.

Israel's army knew this was a miracle of divine intervention. Emboldened by what they had witnessed, they pursued the scattered enemy forces. God's Word tells us, "At Barak's advance, the LORD routed Sisera. . . . All the troops of Sisera fell by the sword; not a man was left" (Judg. 4:15-16). Deborah's word that the honor of Sisera's death would go to a woman was fulfilled when a woman named Jael slew him as he hid. Nevertheless, General Barak could rejoice in his victory. He became a celebrated hero, even listed in the New Testament as a hero of faith (Heb. 11:32).

As for Deborah, on the day of battle she did not flinch. We have no record of whether she actually entered the battlefield. Perhaps, like Moses with his battle against the Amalekites (Ex. 17:10-11), she positioned herself in a visible place above the fighting where the men could see her and take courage from her upraised arms.

In any case, the Lord used Deborah's valiant heart to save the nation. Through her faith and obedience, the Lord utterly and completely routed Israel's enemies. It was a stupendous victory. The land was free again! The people could finally rebuild their lives. God had restored their hope for the future.

Deborah—prophetess, judge, military strategist, warrior, liberator. Add to this, worship leader, songwriter, and historian. Deborah not only initiated the call to fight the oppressors, but she also took the lead in glorifying God for the outcome. This was a great and historic day, and she wanted all of Israel to remember the stunning victory. Proving she could wield both sword and pen, she composed a song that they sang together in grateful commemoration of God's mighty deliverance.

Her song both praised the Lord and offered an important history lesson. During a time when people largely passed down history lessons orally, songs were effective in keeping stories alive and factual. Deborah wrote it in line with the Lord's command: "Only be careful, and watch yourselves closely so that you do not forget the things your eyes have seen or let them slip from your heart as long as you live. Teach them to your children and to their children after them" (Deut. 4:9).

Her hymn of praise and song of victory reviewed and celebrated God's glorious works among them and urged the entire population to join in the celebration. Called the "Song of Deborah," her sublime and immortal song is regarded as one of the oldest portions of the Old Testament and is one of its most beautiful songs.

Those who are valiant in the Lord recognize that it is not by their own strength that they gain victory. Deborah knew how to give God the credit for the victory and take none for herself. In her song, she did not boast but just stated facts, proclaiming God's greatness, reminding the nation of God's faithfulness and character. The hymn reveals all that is in her heart—love for God, reverence, gratitude, awe, praise.

Deborah's valiant heart knew all along that when God is on the march, the earth shakes, the heavens pour, and the mountains quake (Judg. 5:4-5). Indeed, all the forces of nature fight for God. The whole creation, including the very stars, seemed to array themselves with Israel's pitiful little army so that mighty Sisera could do nothing (Judg. 5:20).

The song also gives lessons in national cooperation, commending the tribes that united to defeat the enemy and rebuking those that had failed to join them. (There is no mention of Judah or Simeon among the tribes because they were remote and probably could not get there in time.) For those who were near and yet would not participate, Deborah gives them the shame they deserved.

In this song, we see a final glimpse of Deborah as she describes herself as "a mother in Israel." There is no record that she had natural children of her own. Perhaps she adopted the entire nation as her children. Just as a mother devotes herself to her children's well-being, so Deborah devoted herself to her people's welfare. With all her heart, she bore with her children and provided for their welfare. She strengthened their hearts when they were afraid; she roused them from despair and futility; she energized them to faith.

Deborah's valiant heart was God's gift to the nation in a terrible time of need. Great and small alike heeded her words. She was a strong leader who led the strongest in the land. Her valiant heart inspired faith in Barak. He, too, became a man with a valiant heart.

God's faithful prophetess returned to her palm tree where she ruled Israel in righteousness for forty peaceful years. As the nation's fourth and only female judge to rule, she is among the outstanding women of history. Her brilliant career was due to a valiant heart that trusted God implicitly and would fearlessly obey His every command to the limit of her ability.

Following Deborah's tenure, the nation would slide away from the Lord again. After seven years of enemy oppression, they would repent and see another deliverer. Upon his call, Gideon would claim he was too weak (Judg. 6:15). In the end, however, he would rise to the occasion, becoming a man of valiant heart who triumphed over the enemy. Surely the marvelous stories and the song of Deborah, his predecessor, reassured him. Deborah ends her famous song with these prophetic words: "So may all your enemies perish, O LORD! But may they who love you be like the sun when it rises in its strength" (Judg. 5:31).

Be of good courage, and let us behave ourselves valiantly for our people, and for the cities of our God: and let the LORD do that which is good in his sight.

1 CHRONICLES 19:13 KJV

Through God we shall do valiantly: for he it is that shall tread down our enemies.

PSALM 60:12 KJV

LESSONS FOR OUR OWN HEARTS

My mom was an avid Nelson Eddy/Jeanette MacDonald fan. She owned all of the duo's old musicals and also bought copies for her children. I think of one, a 1935 film entitled *New Moon*, where Eddy plays a French revolutionary. In one memorable scene, he stands among a group of men trying to convince them to recapture their ship. Frightened and complaining that they don't even have guns, they all decline.

Eddy responds, "If I have to, I'll go alone!" Then one man steps forward, and then another, until finally there are ten. Nelson exclaims, "Now we're ten! That makes an army! Who's going to stop us now?" Marching off toward the ship with his men, he leads a rousing song, "Give me some men, who are stouthearted men, who will fight for the right they adore! Start me with ten, who are stouthearted men, and they'll soon give me ten thousand more!" Advancing through the forests toward the ship, their army keeps picking up more men until they have more than enough to win their battle.

Well, here was a scene in Israel where no one fit into the "stouthearted men" category. Wanting an army of ten thousand, the Lord used Deborah instead. She convinced one man, and that one man grew to a conquering army. The difference made by this one woman was astounding.

Before Deborah arose as a "mother in Israel," the nation sang songs of lament, not victory. What kind of songs can we sing over our nation today? Would we have the victory songs of the Lord rise from our land again? We need women like Deborah—women with heroic and valiant hearts to reclaim our land for God. It took a valiant heart to engage a powerful adversary and lead the nation to victory. It took a valiant heart to climb the ranks of men into political, judicial, spiritual, and ultimately military leadership. It took a valiant heart to exercise the various roles of prophetess, judge, arbiter, counselor, teacher, ruler, wife, songwriter, military strategist, national deliverer, and "mother in Israel."

We might look at ourselves and think, *Who am I? God could never use me in such a great way!* But God looks at the heart, and He does not call the equipped; He equips the called. He is more concerned with our availability than with our ability. We can learn a lot from Deborah.

Those whom God uses for great things have learned certain lessons that make them effective. Here are some truths to consider.

Faithfulness in Small Things

I can easily get caught up in the romance of Deborah's story, envisioning her standing defiantly, overlooking the battlefield, tall, erect, hair blowing in the wind, a shield in one hand and a sword in the other. I want to be like her. Snapped back to reality though, I go declare war on my sink full of dirty dishes.

But Deborah's life wasn't always that far removed from ours. She had mundane daily affairs just like the rest of us. She probably kept house, cared for family, and fulfilled civic duties. Before her major assignment, she had proved herself in a thousand ordinary tasks. As she labored under her palm tree, the Lord taught her invaluable lessons that prepared her for greatness. He worked in her wisdom, courage, confidence, faith, and dedication. Her heart grew valiant. One thing led to another. Ascending the ranks of Israel's leadership, she became a "mother" to His people.

So often, however, we want to be faithful in the great things before we have been faithful in the small things. We strive to make it work but end up frustrated. Are you impatient for the Lord to turn you loose on the world? The Lord asks, "Who despises the day of small things?" (Zech. 4:10). Remember the words the Lord longs to tell you one day: "Well done, good and faithful servant. You have been faithful over a little; I will set you over much. Enter into the joy of your master" (Matt. 25:21 ESV).

Relationship with the Lord

One of the first and most strategic battles we must fight is a warfare of intimacy with God. Our mortal enemy, the devil, will do all he can to keep us from winning this one. We have got to learn to put our personal relationship with the Lord first, above all other priorities. Learning to lead a deeply troubled nation was challenging for

Deborah. Nevertheless, she reserved time to be alone with God. Developing a listening ear to His voice, she received a prophetic anointing. While the rest of God's people languished in a confused, impoverished, pitiful state, Deborah gained strength and confidence from walking with God. They saw the problem, but she saw the problem *and* the solution.

Deborah liked life on the heights. She lived, conducted her business, and enjoyed God under her palm tree on a tall hill. Going to war, she climbed Mount Tabor, where from its vantage point she had an unflawed view of the valley below and the heavens above. She saw it all—both the enemy's movements and God's—and she knew God would win.

God says to us all, "Come to the heights with Me—above the swirling clouds of confusion, above your saber-rattling enemies—into My presence. See how great I am and how small they are." On the mountain heights of intimacy with God, where our eyes are fixed on Christ, we see that our risen, victorious Lord can defeat all opposition and, in fact, already has. This is where we come to see and believe that the battle is the Lord's. This is where we receive a valiant heart that no longer fears what people can do to us.

Our enemy wants to draw us down from the heights, alone and without God. Down in the valley, Israel's enemies had great weapons of war. Israel felt defeated, without hope. They cowered before their oppressors. But they didn't have God's perspective. They needed to hear God's truth. They needed to go to the heights, away from the enemy's arena, and hear God's battle plan. Barak had not been with God as Deborah had. To win, he thought he needed her by his side. But she knew better. She already knew who was by their side: "The LORD mighty in battle" (Ps. 24:8).

If you want a valiant heart for the Lord, if you want the anointing, it will come from the Lord. Stay close to Him—hiding yourself in Him, abandoning yourself to His Spirit, seeking Him with all your heart, getting His perspective, hearing His battle plan. The Israelites got into a mess in the first place by losing sight of the Lord and going their own way. They tried to run their lives and solve their problems themselves. But Deborah stayed in contact with the Lord, looking to Him and hearing from Him. Thus she made her decisions based on her walk with Him, a walk that enabled her to conduct all of her affairs brilliantly.

Authority

David cried that the wicked might be "like a slug melting away as it moves along" (Ps. 58:8). Asaph cried that his enemies would be like tumbleweeds that blow right by and disappear (Ps. 83:13). That happened with Deborah's enemies. When she arose as a "mother in Israel," they vanished quickly. Yet she remained, standing tall, like her palm tree: "The righteous will flourish like a palm tree . . ." (Ps. 92:12).

So often though we feel like the slugs and the tumbleweed. How desperately we need a fresh revelation of who we are in Christ! He doesn't just call us to the heights to give us a fresh perspective of what is above and below. He wants us to experience the position of authority that is ours in Christ: "And God raised us up with Christ and seated us with him in the heavenly realms in Christ Jesus" (Eph. 2:6).

As a man, Christ walked in an authority that amazed people. His enemies confronted Him, asking, "Who gave you this authority?" (Mark 1:22, 27; 2:10; Matt. 21:23). He even said that by His authority He could lay down His life and raise it again (John 10:18). Then He shared His authority with His disciples, saying, "I have given you authority . . . to overcome all the power of the enemy" (Luke 10:19; 9:1). In His Great Commission He challenges us, "*All authority* in heaven and on earth has been given to me. Therefore go and make disciples of all nations" (Matt. 28:18-19). In other words: "I have authority over *everything*. I'm imparting it to you. So take the authority and go claim this world for Me."

We are not victims in this world. We are victors, conquerors, people of purpose and victory in an incredible time of destiny. We live on the edge of history. Time is running out, the days are evil, the clouds are darkening, the battle is intensifying, people's hearts are beginning to "faint from fear and foreboding of what is coming upon the world" (Luke 21:26 NRSV). We don't need less authority than the early church knew—we need more! We need to lay claim to the authority Christ made available to us—*all* authority. With His authority, we can stand in full confidence, knowing who we are in the Lord.

Authority comes from believing God's promises—not just in the big things but also in the small. We may not be confronting huge enemy armies, but it takes a valiant heart to see a promise in God's Word and claim it as one's own: "I feel weak and debilitated, but, Lord, I see right here that those who hope in You '*will* renew their strength. They *will* soar on wings like eagles; they *will* run and not grow weary, they *will* walk and not be faint' (Isa. 40:31). That's for me! I claim it! I receive it!" You and I know that it will take a valiant fight of faith to slay the negative doubts that rear up against such a stand.

Deborah's valiant heart looked past the impossible circumstances and believed God's promise. With unflinching faith, she had no trouble stepping out in obedience at God's command. She could cry in faith, "Victory's coming!"

Like other children, my first word was probably "no." Unlike other children though, I think my first sentence was, "I can't." I didn't say it defiantly; I really believed it. But then I learned the power of "I can"—"I can do everything through him who gives me strength" (Phil. 4:13). If we would have valiant hearts, we must spend our energies focusing not on what we cannot do but on what we can do in Him.

We have a choice. Will we walk in the authority that is ours, or will we shirk it? Deborah plowed through the hindrances and barriers that stood in her way. She walked through every door God opened to her. When called upon, she stepped boldly up to the plate. She could sit under her palm issuing decrees, or she could get down in the trenches with the men. Whether settling disputes, proclaiming prophetic words, or mobilizing an army, she would do it for God.

Deborah had a home and family, but she didn't use them as excuses not to use her gifts. She knew that God had given her gifts and that He had called her to use them for the good of His people. In a culture where leaders were generally males, she did not resist or rebel. But neither did she allow her gender to confine or define her either. God chooses leaders by His standards, not ours. His gifts do not carry a gender bias. He will use anyone with a heart for Him. He accomplishes great things through people who allow Him to be great in their hearts. You may not possess "up-front" gifts, but God has gifted you. You have a sphere of influence. Whatever He calls you to do, do it in faith. Do it valiantly and with authority.

Humility

Authority and humility do not oppose each other. In God's kingdom, one without the other is self-defeating. A valiant heart that is not tempered by humility will end up in trouble. Deborah might have become a tyrant had she not been humble. But she was not power hungry; nor did she seek glory or position for herself. Her motive for service was the glory of God and the good of her people. It takes humility to be a truly great leader, and Deborah was humble toward both God and humankind.

Dependence on God might be easier for those with few talents, those who know their inadequacies. People with many talents can easily become self-confident, self-reliant, and proud because they think they can be effective in their own strength. Deborah was multitalented. She was also strong, with great determination and fortitude. But she learned to lay hold of God's strength—not to trust her own. While she showed herself to be adequate in everything she did, she knew the secret to her success was the adequacy of God, not her own. Praise might have come her way, but He got the glory. Despite her varied gifts and abilities, despite her incredible accomplishments, she joyfully pointed to God. We must learn to move in humble dependence upon the Lord's strength alone if we would see victory in our lives. To do anything less endangers us and the commission He has given us.

But true humility also extends to the way we relate to others. We never see Deborah seeking power over people. She did not seek her judgeship. The judges of Israel were people God raised up (Judg. 2:16). They were to lead His people in humility. We see Deborah's humility and eagerness to serve God's people when the need arose. Upon receiving a prophetic promise of the battle's victorious outcome, she, like many of us perhaps, may have been tempted to march out before the army, proudly waving her banner.

But Deborah did not want to lead a parade. She did not look for recognition. Although she was first among her people, she was careful not to usurp Barak's position. She gladly stepped aside for him. Calling him to lead the troops, she challenged him to believe the Lord's promise. She even warned him of consequences if she went with him. Nevertheless, at his request, she did go. In her inspiring song, she praised the Lord for those who willingly took the lead (Judg. 5:2). Clearly, in her mind, this was a victory for which all participants should share recognition.

The way to greatness in God's kingdom is humility. Don't strive to get the credit for your contributions. Simply be a servant. Let God commend you. Let God raise you up, if He chooses, at the right time.

Willingness to Fight

God does not give us authority so we can sit on it. He wants to raise up a warrior generation. He calls us to claim this world for Him. Having declared war and conquered, He wants us to go in His authority, lay hold of His victory, and subdue the enemy. It does not matter whether we think we were recruited or drafted; once we are in God's service, we had better get combat-ready. This is not a time of peace for the church. Whether we like it or not, we are at war. The whole planet is a spiritual battleground. The great conflict of the ages proceeds toward its climax. The time is short. God is issuing no leaves of absence, and He has no reserve troops. He has called us all up for active duty.

Some might see themselves as neutral pacifists, but it won't work because our enemy is not a pacifist. We show our ignorance if we think we can relax in our pews, and the world's troubles will just pass us by. It is foolish to think we can make peace with the devil when he is bent on destroying us and everything for which we stand. The devil will never stand for a truce—nor will God.

When Jesus said, "Blessed are the peacemakers" (Matt. 5:9), He was not talking about taking battle songs like "Onward Christian Soldiers" out of hymnals, as some have done. How Satan loves it! True, God wants us to be reconcilers, to the best of our ability, both on the human level and on the spiritual. But there is an enemy of peace who will resist peace at every hand. As any peacemaker knows, it is a battle to bring peace on earth. We must resist the enemy of peace.

A valiant heart is a warrior heart. Deborah literally led an army, as did Joan of Arc and a few other women down through history. As Christians, however, most of us will never be called upon to fight a war with real guns and bullets. As Paul said, "the weapons of our warfare are not merely human, but they have divine power to destroy strongholds" (2 Cor. 10:4 NRSV). As it fell to Deborah to take the initiative in repelling the Canaanites, it falls to us to rise up in faith against strongholds of sin and Satan. When Jesus told people, "Follow Me," He was recruiting them to come follow Him in His fight for lost souls and a lost world. He was enlisting them to enter the war against Satan's kingdom, to see the kingdom of heaven established on earth.

Sometimes we draw back from fear of conflict. Before going to conquer the Promised Land, Moses instructed the army officers to ask their men, "Is any man afraid or fainthearted? Let him go home so that his brothers will not become disheartened too" (Deut. 20:8). A man without a valiant heart was not fit for the battlefield. Also he might discourage the others and keep them from claiming their inheritance, too. We have not been offered a similar option of staying home today. God wants us to arise, strengthen and establish our own hearts, and fearlessly enter the battle. As we do this, we will strengthen the hearts of others, too.

Don't let fear or apathy conquer you. With valiant heart, renounce these enemies. We can mask timidity with false humility, saying, "I'm just a woman." We can stay home and do little to advance God's kingdom and feel quite self-righteous about our noninvolvement. We can avoid the newspaper or TV news and feel quite holy as we remain ignorant of the need for our prayers and involvement in the world. But how can we pray effectively, how can we win the war, if we withdraw from the field?

Sometimes our life, even apart from spiritual considerations, seems like a war zone at home, on the job, and even at church. Emotionally, we feel as if we are suffering from shellshock and battle fatigue, ready for a Purple Heart. But it's not time to raise the white flag. It's time to reclaim your authority, to put on the armor of God (Eph. 6:13-18), rally the troops, and march out in faith with a valiant heart. We must not give up our agonizing prayers for our family or our efforts to win our neighbors to Jesus. We must never give our church, our city, or our nation up to the devil. Deborah did not doubt that the Lord would help her win the victory. And He will help us win *our* victories, too!

It takes a valiant heart to go out and fight the Lord's battles with grace. Though we get tired and wounded, our eyes must remain firmly fixed on Jesus, our Commander in Chief. We declare, "I renounce this weak, wimpy, sniveling spirit. I renounce this faint heart, and I receive a valiant heart. By faith I receive the Spirit's life and power. I put on the garments of praise. In Jesus' name, I am more than a conqueror, and I will never accept defeat!"

Don't we get tired and need rest? Of course, we do. But our rest is not a careless rest that leaves us exposed. Even our rest is part of the war. It is a fight to rest in the Lord—meditating on His Word, quietly singing His songs, praying, seeking His presence. Don't we also need to play and have fun? Yes, but even that includes warfare. Who doesn't know that some of the worst battles in the family often take place on family vacations or during leisure time? There is just no escaping the war.

Deborah shows us what a woman can do when God has complete control of her life. She decided that some things are worth dying for. Without regard for her own safety, she marched into battle. Her valiant heart proved the literal truth of Joshua's words: "One of you routs a thousand, because the LORD your God fights for you, just as he promised" (Josh. 23:10).

Many of God's people today need to be aroused by Deborahs. You may not be a prominent leader, but with God's help, you can rise to the occasion and assert leadership nonetheless. God wants to use us to awaken the hearts of His people from their flagging spiritual condition. He wants to use us to help them face and win their difficult battles, to stir them to arise and put on God's strength, to lay claim to the power and authority available to them in Christ, and to encourage them to go forth boldly into triumph. When you see the needs, will you say, "Lord, send me"?

To motivate her people to go to war, Deborah not only laid out the battle plan, but she went to war herself. Her valiant heart fostered faith in Barak. The Lord needs brave-hearted women like Deborah today to rise up from across our land—warriors who will rely on His Spirit's power, who will smash through life's impossible challenges, who will deliver His people and bring the nation back from the brink of ruin.

Christ is worthy! So let us fight to see His kingdom come and His will be done on earth as it is in heaven (Matt. 6:10)! Resolve to be one of those who will "not love their lives so much as to shrink from death" (Rev. 12:11). You will rejoice when you see your victorious Savior and King come riding through the heavens on His white horse, followed by the armies of heaven (Rev. 19:11-16).

The LORD will march out like a mighty man, like a warrior he will stir up his zeal; with a shout he will raise the battle cry and will triumph over his enemies.

ISAIAH 42:13

Perseverance

Being valiant is not limited to one decisive thrust. We may get excited over some new program and gladly jump on board. After exerting some effort—fasting, praying, having an outreach—we are glad when "it's over." We think, *There! I've done it. Now I can get back to normal.* But wait a minute! We have done little more than establish a beachhead, a starting point. We've got to have a commitment to see the operation through to the end. We must keep moving until we see the enemy completely defeated. If not, he will just be like the tide that washes back in and ruins the precious little sand castle we just built.

Deborah had made such a commitment. She won the great battle, but her task did not start or finish there. She was a history-changer but not because of the one big event. It was also historic that she led the nation through its dark hours of apostasy. Who knows how many years before that large battle she had faithfully spoken God's Word to her people, preparing them for the repentance it would take to see relief from their bondage. Because of her faith, she changed the course of the nation. Then through another forty years of her leadership, the nation enjoyed peace. What a tribute to Deborah's ongoing wise leadership!

Through all the years she remained true to the Lord's larger call on her life—to lead her people. While other women were home mending their clothes, she was mending the nation; while other women fought the battle of maintaining a disciplined home life, she fought the battle for the nation's deliverance. If the Lord had led her to stay home, she would have done that gladly. But God called her to lead, and lead she did, with a wholehearted dedication to complete the task.

When God chose to answer the repentant nation's prayers and

free the people from the tyranny of their oppressors, He looked under Deborah's palm tree for a chosen instrument. Will the Lord look at your address? Wouldn't you love your home, your friends, your neighbors, your church, your town, your world to enjoy forty years of peace? Would you, like Deborah, use your gifts and not bury your talents in the ground? Would you be "a mother" to God's people—a spiritual mother—to bring wisdom, guidance, hope; to challenge, direct, encourage; to bring the Word of the Lord to His distressed and defeated people? God particularly chose Deborah to guide His struggling and stubborn people, but we, too, are chosen. The Holy Spirit is in us. We can receive guidance from the Lord. We can be a prophetic voice in our world.

God is looking for Deborahs in these end times—for those who know their God, who have faith in Him, and who will believe Him for the impossible. He seeks those who are willing to be His voice, who will offer leadership in resolving thorny issues, and who will contend for the faith without being contentious. He wants Deborahs who will march into battle valiantly, fight the good fight victoriously, sing songs of triumph joyfully, finish their course faithfully—knowing He is with them.

You may feel like an ordinary woman, but God can use ordinary women in mighty ways. Deborah was an ordinary woman until God raised her to greatness. God will choose anyone to accomplish His purpose—young or old, male or female, oppressed or free—who will stand with God in faith. If a woman has a valiant heart of faith, God will do the rest, even wonders she never dreamed possible.

May the Lord raise up Deborahs in our midst today—women who can exhibit valiant hearts in an hour where there are many foes and challenges. May you be one of them.

Heart Check

1. Do you think Deborah's calling ever pushed her past her personal comfort zone? How do you think she responded?

2. Do you need a more valiant heart? How can you aim to be more like Deborah?

3. What practical principles have you learned from Deborah? How can you apply them?

4. How can you encourage others in God's army?

5. Compose a prayer to God in response to this chapter's lessons.

5

Queen Esther

THE DARING HEART

BOOK OF ESTHER

SHE WAS ONE OF the most stunningly beautiful women in the Persian Empire. Since winning the royal beauty contest for queen a few years back, she had relaxed into a pampered lifestyle in the sumptuous palace. Now shaken from her complacency, she felt as if the sky had fallen. Her people—thousands of innocent Jews—would soon be savagely wiped from the earth. Not only that, despite her youth and inexperience, she was the one who must save them.

Adorned in her most royal robes, decked in her finest jewels, Queen Esther looked exquisite. Beneath all the pomp and glitter, however, beat the heart of a young woman who feared for her life. She tried hard to mask it, but her dark, exotic eyes betrayed her. Trying to walk straight and tall, she marched bravely through the long hall toward the king's forbidding throne room. Yes, she was his wife, but the most powerful man on earth had already proved that a wife who crossed him meant little to him. Was this her death march? She would soon know.

Esther could have made the easy choice. But recognizing her duty, she decided that, if necessary, she would die trying to save her people. She risked it all—her husband, her title, her life. We call Esther's heart The Daring Heart.

Esther's husband, King Xerxes (pronounced Zurk-seez; Hebrew: Ahasuerus), wasn't just any ordinary potentate. As sovereign ruler of the Persian Empire—the dominant superpower then—all its power and authority centered in him. The largest empire of the ancient Near East, it stretched from India to Ethiopia (Cush), incorporating the 127 provinces of Media and Persia, as well as the former empires of Assyria and Babylon. Known as "Xerxes the Great," this Persian king was the son of Darius I (Hystaspes) and Atossa, daughter of Cyrus. Xerxes succeeded to the throne of his father in 486 B.C. at about the age of thirty-five. Before this, he had ruled for a dozen years as the governor in Babylonia, which had fallen to Persia.

From Persian documents, we learn a lot about this king. He was an autocrat whose will was absolute. Holding the power of life and death for all his subjects, he ruled with a heavy hand. As seen by his military invasions, his move against his former queen, Vashti, and other activities, we find a proud, impulsive, temperamental, and unpredictable man. One historian calls him arrogant, unstable, savage, ultimately weak, and of poor judgment.

Preparing to invade Greece, Xerxes held a huge banquet in the third year of his reign at his lavish winter royal residence in Susa (or Shushan, a citadel in modern southwestern Iran). Lasting 180 days, this banquet consolidated support for his war effort among his military officers, noblemen, and provincial officials. He culminated this event with a weeklong banquet for everyone in Susa. On the final day, drunk and not thinking clearly, the king ordered his queen, Vashti, to appear unveiled before the crowd to show off her beauty. She refused to comply with this shameful request. Furious, the king consulted his advisers and then deposed her.

Soon after this Xerxes went to war, leading some 360,000 or more men plus a thousand ships, in hopes of conquering Greece. He suffered crushing defeats and returned home battle-weary and licking his wounds. His ego had been badly bruised, and perhaps he felt depressed and lonely. It had been several years since he had deposed his fair queen, but he could not get her out of his mind. He knew he had acted impulsively in a face-saving move against her, and he may have become full of remorse. However, not only had he punished her, but he had enacted an irrevocable law against her. Though he would have been happy for a reconciliation, he had no power to undertake it.

His counselors wanted him to forget Vashti, and they had an idea. They would send representatives throughout the kingdom to search for beautiful young virgins and bring these to the harem in Susa. After receiving royal beauty treatments, this array of gorgeous virgins could entertain the king until he found the right one to crown as his new queen. Xerxes agreed to the plan. So his officers fanned out all over the kingdom to find the loveliest candidates. Soon young women were coming into the king's harem from all over the empire—according to Josephus, some four hundred of them.

Before we get romantic notions about this contest for the crown of "Miss Persia," we should look at the facts. Here beauty was a definite liability, because Persian kings collected beautiful women the way they collected jewels. Some of these young girls must have felt horror as they were rounded up and carried away from their homes to live a secluded life in a harem. True, they would have every luxury, and for twelve months they would go through extensive "makeovers." (Most of us would jump for joy over a simple three-hour professional makeover.) This intense beautification program would include such things as ritual cleansings, the removal of body hair, elaborate skin treatments that included lighteners, elegant makeup, and exotic perfumes.

Yet despite all this fuss, the women would be mere chattel, enslaved with no hope of freedom. Serving as sexual partners at the king's pleasure, their only purpose in life would be to await his call. He would keep them as secondary wives, providing for them, but they could never marry. There was one sliver of hope for these women though. One of them would become the queen of the Persian Empire.

According to the contest's rules, each night a different contestant would spend the night with the king and leave in the morning. After her one-night stand, she would go to another part of the harem to await her fate. She could no longer go to the section reserved for virgins. But woe to the losers! Unless a woman pleased the king immensely, she would likely be forgotten, destined to become a lifelong recluse in the harem. We can only imagine then the level of competition and infighting among these women as they vied for the position of queen.

Right there in Susa lived a Jewish exile named Mordecai whom King Nebuchadnezzar of Babylon had carried away from Jerusalem before Babylon passed to Persian control. Xerxes' forebear, Cyrus, had given the Jews freedom to emigrate back to Jerusalem, but Mordecai had elected to stay in Persia, along with many of his people who had lived and prospered there.

It so happened that Mordecai had a niece named Hadassah (Hebrew for "myrtle") whom he had raised since her childhood. When the girl was orphaned, he took her as his own daughter, loving her with all the affection of a father for his only child. Part of adapting to their new environment meant taking on Persian names. A lovely child, Hadassah was given the name Esther, meaning "star."

Esther was one of the beautiful young women chosen for the great contest. We don't know whether she went willingly or was dragged. Regardless, it must have been a wrenching experience for her and Mordecai. Once inside the harem, she was entrusted to the care of Hegai (the king's eunuch), who had charge of the women. Hegai took an instant liking to Esther. In fact, he made her his special project, giving her preferential treatment—special food and beauty treatments, seven maids to care for her needs, and the best place in the harem. With Hegai's special grooming, Esther was the odds-on favorite.

Mordecai and Esther had such a deep bond of love that he spent each day walking back and forth near the harem to hear news of her welfare. For her part, she trusted him implicitly and always obeyed him even in his absence. He told her not to reveal her nationality or family background to anyone, and she complied.

When it was Esther's turn to appear before the king, Hegai advised her what to take with her—what jewels and clothing to wear, what tokens, what instrumentalists. She asked for nothing more than what he advised. This was the moment for which she had waited an entire year, and she was ready.

Esther was a smash hit with Xerxes. Her physical charms no doubt captivated him, but beyond this shone a uniqueness, an inner beauty that the outer merely adorned. This was a woman of surpassing loveliness—beauty of form, personality, character—that distanced her from all her rivals. Forgetting all his former woes and every other woman, after one short night, he fell in love with her.

Such a situation violates God's demands for sexual purity, and the Bible does not explain why He allowed Esther to spend the night with Xerxes as part of His plan. Nevertheless, He fulfilled His larger purpose. Xerxes immediately set a crown on Esther's head. She was the new queen, and everyone in the court who saw her also approved of her. To introduce his queen, he gave another lavish banquet for all of his nobles and officials. The celebration lasted many days, during which Xerxes also proclaimed a national holiday and distributed gifts liberally throughout the kingdom.

What a momentous victory for Esther! Still, she could not rejoice without fear. Even as queen, she would have few rights. Surely during her time in the harem, she had heard many whispers about her new husband. How would she feel, knowing that she had just married a ruthless egomaniac who had ousted her predecessor for not letting herself be paraded before a pack of lustful men? How would she feel, knowing that a harem full of women waited in the background to take her place if she made a misstep? Esther would definitely want to tread her Persian rugs very cautiously.

Meanwhile Mordecai had become an official of some sort, perhaps by Esther's recommendation. He sat at the king's gate (a place like city hall where much business takes place). This was a great place for picking up tidbits of news about Esther, and one day he overheard something alarming: Two palace guards were plotting to assassinate the king! He immediately sent word to Esther, who reported it to the king, giving Mordecai the credit. When it was found to be true, they hanged the two conspirators and duly recorded Mordecai's deed in the Book of the Chronicles, an ancient court diary of memorable events.

A number of years passed, and Mordecai was never rewarded. In time a man named Haman gained Xerxes' favor. In fact, Haman so impressed the king that he elevated him high above all his other nobles, to his second-in-command. Since he was the king's favored friend, confidant, and prime minister, everyone in the kingdom—great and small alike—knelt in homage before Haman whenever he passed. That is, everyone except Mordecai.

Mordecai could not bring himself to pay homage to the man. He realized that Haman expected more than allegiance. He wanted worship, something Mordecai refused to give any mere mortal. The first commandment strictly charges God's people not to worship anyone but Him, and Mordecai viewed bowing to Haman as an act of worship.

Other officials began to question Mordecai's behavior, asking him, "Why do you disobey the king's command?" (Est. 3:3). Mordecai would explain that it went against his Jewish faith. They kept pressing him. Finally they went to Haman to see if a Jew would get a special dispensation. But Haman had no heart for the Jews. He was an Agagite—a descendant of the Amalekites, ancient enemies of Israel (see Deut. 25:17-19)—whose very name means "warlike."

Proud and pampered, Haman stood at the pinnacle of power in the empire. How dare a peon like Mordecai not properly honor him! Such flagrant disrespect stung his ego. He would not be happy until Mordecai licked his feet.

Haman's quest for power and his hatred of the Jews made a deadly mix. Destroying Mordecai was not enough. He must destroy all he stood for—a people whose dedication to God stood in the way of the reverence he wanted for himself. Mordecai represented a whole race that would never honor Haman properly. They looked to the Lord as their highest authority, not to him; so he must stamp them all out, the entire Jewish race. Full of bitter determination, he set to work. Haman was smart, shrewd, fervid about his tasks, and tremendously malevolent and devious. In no time he had devised an airtight plan. Every Jew soon would be caught in his web and eradicated.

The first thing Haman did was to seek the advice of the court astrologers and magicians about when to kill the Jews. Casting lots (Persian: *pur*), he decided his diabolical plot should take place one year later, in the month of Adar (March). Next he went to Xerxes. Feigning concern for the king's interests, he began a speech all too familiar to Jews: "There is a certain people dispersed and scattered among the peoples in all the provinces of your kingdom whose customs are different from those of all other people and who do not obey the king's laws; it is not in the king's best interest to tolerate them" (Est. 3:8).

Blending truth and error, Haman had described these "certain people"—too insignificant to name and yet too dangerous to ignore—as living by a different set of laws from the rest of his subjects, laws that disregarded and undermined the king's authority. Concluding his case, he said, "If it pleases the king, let a decree be issued to destroy them, and I will put ten thousand talents of silver into the royal treasury for the men who carry out this business" (Est. 3:9). This was an enormous sum of money. An Old Testament talent was a unit of weight equivalent to about 75.6 pounds; so his offer was about 378 tons of silver.[1]

Haman had laid out his plan well, and he could not have hoped for a better response. To his surprise, Xerxes was so fond of his prime minister and so grateful for his eye for order in the empire that he would not think of taking this sum from him. So trusting was he that he didn't even bother to find out who these troublesome people were. So heartless was he that he didn't even care that a whole group of his subjects was scheduled to die. Satisfied to leave the affair to Haman, he took his signet ring from his finger and handed it to him. "Keep the money," he said, "and do with the people as you please" (Est. 3:11).

The king's signet ring bearing his official seal was the equivalent of the king's own signature. He had given Haman unlimited power to pass whatever decree he wished in his name. Sealing an edict against the Jews with this ring would seal their fate. Haman left the king's presence at once to draw up his bloody edict. Summoning the royal secretaries, he had them copy, translate, and send the documents, stamped with the king's signet, to all corners of the empire.

Now he could savor his victory. He had fixed his wicked plan irrevocably into law. No one—not even the king himself—could change a royal edict. Within eight weeks all the good citizens of the empire would receive word to "destroy, kill and annihilate all the Jews—young and old, women and little children—on a single day, the thirteenth day of the twelfth month, the month of Adar [March 7, 473 B.C.], and to plunder their goods" (Est. 3:13).

If Haman had intended to have all Jews banished, it would have been bad enough. But so cruel was he that he ordered the merciless murders of innocent men, women, and children without even showing cause. Considering the scope of the empire, his plot virtually meant the extinction of the Jewish race—his express intention.

The residents of Susa received the edict with bewilderment. Xerxes and Haman, however, celebrated the occasion by boozing it up together. Little did Xerxes know that his ring had signed his own queen's death warrant.

Throughout the provinces, Jews responded to the staggering news with deep grief. Mordecai, likewise, was horrified. He had no temple to mourn at, and so he publicly mourned—tearing his clothes, putting on sackcloth, smearing himself with ashes, and wailing loudly in the city streets.

Meanwhile Esther sat in the palace, secluded from affairs of state. News of the heinous crime being perpetrated against her people had escaped her. Soon, however, she heard about Mordecai's shocking behavior. The news distressed her greatly. She sent him a set of clothes to put on, but Mordecai refused them and kept on wailing in the streets.

This perturbed Esther even more. *What is going on?* she wondered. *I've never seen Mordecai behave like this.* She could not rest until she got to the bottom of it. But so strictly did Persian laws confine wives, especially those of the king, that Mordecai and Esther could not talk openly. She immediately sent her servant Hathach to find out what had so deeply troubled her uncle.

Esther didn't know that her inquiry would bring about the greatest challenge of her life. Mordecai explained everything to Hathach, handing him a copy of the edict for Esther to read. He sent an appeal to her that she approach the king and implore him for mercy on behalf of her people. Hathach returned to the palace and reported to her all that Mordecai had said.

When Esther heard the news, she could not have been more shocked. Her husband had ordered the extermination of all the Jews in the kingdom? How could it be? But here was the evidence. She didn't know what to do, and Mordecai's request terrified her. She had always followed his instructions, including continuing to keep her nationality a secret. But Persian royals were obliged to marry wives from one of Persia's great families, which she was not. Xerxes, thinking she was Persian through and through, had never asked about her pedigree; nor had she offered it. Now Mordecai asked her to go to the king for "her people" (Est. 4:8).

Many thoughts must have run through Esther's mind at this point. *What can I do? Xerxes doesn't even know I'm Jewish! I've got to confess that I am one of those he has doomed? How will he react?* Even before this crisis, she may have been fighting feelings of insecurity, for he had not called to see her in over a month. She may have wondered, *Where do I stand? Have I fallen out of favor? Does he still love me, or has another woman caught his fancy?* But there was a worse possibility. *What if Haman learned about me and went to him? What if Xerxes intends to kill me?*

One might think that as queen of an empire, Esther would have felt more confident of her position. But she feared her husband greatly, knowing she possessed a crown and a title but few rights. Xerxes might view her more as a glorified harem girl, easily replaceable, than as his wife and queen.

Add to these fears, her fear of exacerbating any problems. She had never been anything but compliant—compliant with Mordecai, compliant with Hegai, compliant with Xerxes. She definitely was not a rule-breaker and had never stepped out of line. The king had deposed the former queen for her disrespect, and Esther did not want to make a similar mistake.

Haman was a wicked man, but Xerxes was not much better. Everyone in the kingdom could live or die at his whim. And now Mordecai had urged Esther to break one of the court's cardinal rules. The king protected himself by not allowing anyone, not even the queen, to enter his presence without his summons. If someone approached him that he did not care to see, he could order the person's immediate execution by refusing to raise his golden scepter. The Greek historian Herodotus says that when Xerxes sat on his throne, men with axes in their hands stood around him, ready to punish any who approached without being called.

When a king's face brightens, it means life; his favor is like a rain cloud in spring.

PROVERBS 16:15

A king's wrath is like the roar of a lion; he who angers him forfeits his life.

PROVERBS 20:2

Even with her favored position, approaching the king in this way meant Esther would risk her life. And she knew that the one who ruled 127 provinces had trouble ruling his own temper. He had banished Vashti, and any attempt by her ever to approach him again would bring her certain death. This was all too much. After all, Esther had been groomed as a showpiece, not a mouthpiece. How could she go to Xerxes and convince him to reverse lofty Haman's decree? It seemed impossible.

Esther sent a reply to Mordecai explaining, "All the king's servants and the people of the king's provinces know that if any man or woman goes to the king inside the inner court without being called, there is but one law—all alike are to be put to death. Only if the king holds out the golden scepter to someone, may that person live. I myself have not been called to come into the king for thirty days" (Est. 4:11 NRSV).

If Esther thought Mordecai would appreciate her dilemma, she was disappointed. He sent back a stern appeal, warning Esther, "Do not think that because you are in the king's house you alone of all the Jews will escape. For if you remain silent at this time, relief and deliverance for the Jews will arise from another place, but you and your father's family will perish. *And who knows but that you have come to royal position for such a time as this?*" (Est. 4:13-14, emphasis mine).

Such challenging words for the ears of the young, sheltered, inexperienced queen to whom the affairs of state, heretofore, had been of no interest. But now Mordecai even suggested that God had raised her to her position for this very hour of crisis.

Receiving this message, Esther knew she had to make a choice. She could conceal her ethnic identity and hope to live the rest of her life as a pampered queen, or she could risk her life by trying to save her people. Mordecai's words rang true in her heart. God had not given her this favored position of queen for her own benefit. With the privilege came a responsibility. Her people were in peril, and she must try to save them.

She had never thought of herself as bold, but she was about to prove her mettle. God was giving her a daring heart to do His will. Although she trembled at her decision, a firmness, a resoluteness, stirred within her. For the first time, she would take on the mantle of leader, protector, and deliverer. She could not count on the king's favor; nor could she underestimate the ruthlessness of his second-in-command. Yet with daring heart, she would risk her reputation, her position, and her life. Contrary to the law, she would go before the king and plead for the lives of her people, no matter how it ended for her.

She recognized, however, that she needed spiritual support for such a mission. She needed God's strength and wisdom and the right strategy. So she sent a reply to Mordecai, directing him, "Go, gather together all the Jews who are in Susa, and fast for me. Do not eat or drink for three days, night or day. I and my maids will fast as you do. When this is done, I will go to the king, even though it is against the law. And if I perish, I perish" (4:16).

Mordecai followed Esther's instructions, and Esther also prayed, fasted, planned, and prepared. On the third day, she donned her royal robes. Her palms were probably sweaty and her body tense, but she had a daring heart that propelled her on her mission. First, she conquered the inner court; then she moved to the entrance of the king's throne room. It was awesome, resembling a Grecian temple, and she could see Xerxes sitting on his magnificent throne at the end. Keeping her composure as best she could, she stopped and waited. She could see his scepter. How would he use it? He looked up. She bowed . . . and waited.

Suddenly Xerxes took his scepter in hand and extended it toward her, indicating that she might approach him. So she drew near and touched the top of the scepter. She saw the warmth in his eyes. He was happy to see her. He was so pleased, in fact, that he asked, "What is it, Queen Esther? What is your request? Even up to half the kingdom, it will be given you" (Est. 5:3). Her life was spared! What relief! What an answer to prayer!

But this was only the first hurdle. Xerxes knew she had come with a request and seemed eager to fill it. Yet she must not act hastily. She was dealing with powerful diabolic forces and needed to tread carefully, for she had not yet revealed her Jewish identity. Knowing how Xerxes loved to eat, she had prepared a feast for the king and Haman. There was nothing like a sumptuous meal to soften his heart before she revealed her true purpose. "If it pleases the king," she said humbly and sweetly to him, "let the king, together with Haman, come today to a banquet I have prepared for him" (Est. 5:4).

It did please the king. He dropped everything immediately and ordered his servants, "Bring Haman at once, so that we may do what Esther asks" (Est. 5:5). So Xerxes and his prime minister were soon doing what they loved best—drinking wine and feasting—at Esther's dinner party.

Xerxes was discerning enough to know that Esther had something significant on her mind. More than a bit curious, he asked, "Now what is your petition? It will be given you. And what is your request? Even up to half the kingdom, it will be granted" (Est. 5:6).

Sensing that this was not the most opportune time, she asked no more of Xerxes than a promise to accept another invitation for the next day. "If the king regards me with favor and if it pleases the king to grant my petition and fulfill my request, let the king and Haman come tomorrow to the banquet I will prepare for them. Then I will answer the king's question" (Est. 5:8).

Xerxes liked this intriguing game of cat and mouse, and he quickly accepted this second invitation. Haman likewise was thrilled at these exclusive dinners with the king and queen. If he had been full of himself before, he now gushed with self-adulation. He couldn't wait to get home to tell his friends and family.

Leaving the grounds, however, Haman saw Mordecai sitting at the king's gate. As usual Mordecai failed to show him the least bit of respect, neither rising nor bowing before him. Haman was furious! But he would deal with this insubordinate later. For now he had another matter to attend to. He went home and called for all of his friends and his wife, Zeresh. Once he had a good audience, he proceeded to boast about his vast wealth, his many sons, and all the ways Xerxes had honored him above everyone else. Then he exulted, "And that's not all! I'm the only person Queen Esther invited to accompany the king to the banquet she gave. And she has invited me along with the king tomorrow" (Est. 5:12).

But the same overweening pride that caused him to boast over his good fortune also spoiled his exultation. Smoldering over Mordecai's slight to his authority, he lamented, "But all this gives me no satisfaction as long as I see that Jew Mordecai sitting at the king's gate" (Est. 5:13).

So Zeresh and his guests advised him, "Have a gallows built, seventy-five feet high, and ask the king in the morning to have Mordecai hanged on it. Then go with the king to the dinner and be happy" (5:14). What a great idea! Hanging Mordecai from such a height would not only disgrace his memory, but would serve as a grim reminder to the entire city of what becomes of those who show disrespect to Haman. He resolved to have the gallows built first thing in the morning.

But that night a strange thing happened. While Haman lay plotting Mordecai's demise, the king could not sleep. So in trying to think of a way to get sleepy, he had his servants stay up and read to him from the Book of the Chronicles, a royal record of the events of his reign. It was almost dawn when the sleepy king sat up straight. "Wait! Back up! Read that again!" They had just read how Mordecai had saved his life some years back by foiling the assassination plot against him. They read it to him again.

"What honor and recognition has Mordecai received for this?" he asked.

They searched the account. "Nothing has been done for him," they answered (Est. 6:3).

What? This bureaucratic blunder must be corrected! Persian

kings were quick to honor subjects who demonstrated this kind of loyalty, and Xerxes would see this heroic patriot duly rewarded—at once!

Meanwhile the sun was rising, and Haman, impatient to carry out his own plans for Mordecai, intended to be first to see the king before other business got in the way of his own. All he needed was for Xerxes to sign Mordecai's death warrant, a simple thing. After all, Haman always got what he wanted—even an order to exterminate a whole race of people. Upon his arrival at the court he felt confident. It was going to be a great day!

But little did Haman know that his plot was already unraveling under the sovereign hand of God. Just as he had designed to destroy Mordecai, God had put it in the heart of Xerxes to honor Mordecai. Both were impatient to see their objectives accomplished expeditiously. Noticing someone standing in the court, Xerxes asked his servants, "Who is in the court?" (Est. 6:4).

"Haman is standing in the court," they replied.

He was delighted to hear it was Haman. Who, after all, was wiser than Haman? Haman would know how best to honor Mordecai.

"Bring him in," he ordered (Est. 6:5).

Haman was pleased to be called in so quickly. Before he could open his mouth to express his business though, Xerxes asked, "What should be done for the man the king delights to honor?"

What! This so startled Haman that he almost forgot Mordecai. *Who is there that the king would rather honor than me?* he thought (Est. 6:6). He craved adoration—the thing Mordecai refused him—more than anything else Xerxes could offer him.

He didn't even have to think about his answer. He already knew what further recognition he would like for himself. It would be extravagant, the kind of honor reserved for royalty, but not too great for Haman. He quickly replied, "For the man the king delights to honor, have them bring a royal robe the king has worn and a horse the king has ridden, one with a royal crest placed on its head. Then let the robe and horse be entrusted to one of the king's most noble princes. Let them robe the man the king delights to honor, and lead him on the horse through the city streets, proclaiming before him, 'This is what is done for the man the king delights to honor!'"(Est. 6:7-9).

Xerxes thought it was a *great* idea! "Go at once," the king ordered him. "Get the robe and the horse and do just as you have suggested for *Mordecai the Jew*, who sits at the king's gate. Do not neglect anything you have recommended" (Est. 6:10, emphasis mine).

No, not Mordecai! There must be some mistake! Not his bitter enemy! Haman was utterly astounded and crushed, but he must comply. Miserable, he put a royal robe on Mordecai and paraded him throughout the city streets on Xerxes' own horse, proclaiming, "This is what is done for the man the king delights to honor!" (Est. 6:11). Afterward Mordecai returned to the king's gate, but Haman rushed home with his head covered in grief and shame.

However, this devastating humiliation would be the least of his troubles. Persians used signs and omens to forecast future events, and when he reported his woes to Zeresh and his advisers—those who had urged him to take vengeance on Mordecai—they changed their tune. Now predicting that he could never prosper in a plot against the Jews, they said, "Since Mordecai, before whom your downfall has started, is of Jewish origin, you cannot stand against him—you will surely come to ruin!" (Est. 6:13).

Before Haman could recover from these blows, royal escorts came and whisked him away to Esther's banquet. Surely he had lost all appetite for food and fellowship. As the three dined together a second time, they were drinking wine when Xerxes posed the question on his heart. "Queen Esther, what is your petition? It will be given you. What is your request? Even up to half the kingdom, it will be granted" (Est. 7:2). This was the third time he had promised her whatever she wanted, and she knew he was in earnest. *This is it!* she thought. *The time will never be better. Lord, grant me favor!*

With daring heart, Esther said, "If I have found favor with you, O king, and if it pleases your majesty, grant me my life—this is my petition. And spare my people—this is my request. For I and my people have been sold for destruction and slaughter and annihilation. If we had merely been sold as male and female slaves, I would have kept quiet, because no such distress would justify disturbing the king" (Est. 7:3-4).

What! Xerxes could not have been more shocked. He would have given his queen half the kingdom—jewels, land, buildings, slaves— anything. Instead she pleaded for her life like a criminal. Who would dare to plot the murder of his queen and her people? "Who is he?" he asked irately. "Where is the man who has dared to do such a thing?" (Est. 7:5).

This was the moment Esther had waited for. God had trained her hands for war, her fingers for battle (Ps. 144:1). Boldly pointing her finger directly into Haman's face, she declared, "The adversary and enemy is this vile Haman" (Est. 7:6).

Xerxes suddenly understood the link between Esther's appeal and Haman's plot. He stormed from the palace into his garden to cool off and consider his options. He was furious with Haman but no doubt with himself, too. How could his prime minister have so abused his position? As for himself, how could he have made this villainous man his closest adviser and highest-ranking official? How could he have been so foolishly duped into dooming his own queen, not to mention an entire race of innocent people?

Haman was terrified. Now the haughty prosecutor had become the prosecuted. He fell on Esther's couch where she sat and frantically begged for her mercy. But his desperate appeal for his life would only make matters worse. Xerxes returned to a scene that looked to him like Haman pawing Esther. His fury boiled over as he bellowed, "Will he even molest the queen while she is with me in the house?" (Est. 7:8). He now saw double reasons to order Haman's execution.

The king's servants had worshiped Haman as a rising sun but

were quick to abandon him as a falling star. They now felt free, even happy, to inform Xerxes of the gallows Haman had built for Mordecai. One of them offered, "A gallows seventy-five feet high stands by Haman's house. He had it made for Mordecai, who spoke up to help the king" (Est. 7:9).

If the king had felt a smidgeon of leniency, this new bit of evidence ruined it. Haman had prepared a gallows for the man whom the king had delighted to honor as a hero, the man who had saved his life. Haman's fate was sealed completely. "Hang him on it!" he roared (Est. 7:9). So they hanged Haman on the very gallows he had prepared for Mordecai.

How the mighty had fallen. He who would sacrifice a whole people for revenge had become the object of divine retribution. Xerxes was as satisfied in seeing Haman hanged as he had been in seeing Mordecai honored. How truly spoken are the words: "He who digs a hole and scoops it out falls into the pit he has made. The trouble he causes recoils on himself; his violence comes down on his own head" (Ps. 7:15-16).

Xerxes confiscated Haman's estate and gave it to Esther that day. After she revealed her relationship with Mordecai, Xerxes promoted him, giving him all the power, possessions, and prestige that Haman had enjoyed. He even presented him with his signet ring, royal garments, and a large gold crown.

But Esther's work was not over. Her people were still doomed because the edict against them remained in force. Since Persians believed their kings to be gods, a king's edict sealed with his signet ring was considered infallible and, therefore, immutable. A divine king would never make a mistake!

So with daring heart, Esther came before Xerxes a second time without being called. This time she fell at his feet, weeping and pleading. He extended his gold scepter, and she stood up and said, "If it pleases the king . . . let an order be written overruling the dispatches that Haman . . . devised and wrote to destroy the Jews in all the king's provinces. For how can I bear to see disaster fall on my people? How can I bear to see the destruction of my family?" (Est. 8:5-6).

His heart went out to her, and he instructed Esther and Mordecai to devise another decree on behalf of the Jews to counteract the first one and to seal it with his ring. This second decree was drawn up and sent to all who received the first one, including the Jews and officials of every province. It granted Jews in every city the right to defend themselves from their enemies on the appointed day of their extermination. As a result, the city of Susa held a joyous celebration: "When the righteous prosper, the city rejoices; when the wicked perish, there are shouts of joy" (Prov. 11:10). Jews throughout the empire rejoiced and celebrated with feasting. People of many nationalities became Jews because they now held the Jews in high honor.

On the appointed day, many enemies whom the first edict had aroused hoped they could overpower the Jews and seize their holdings. But the tables had turned since officials throughout the kingdom, fearing Mordecai, helped the Jews. The day originally marked for their doom turned out to be the day their enemies perished instead. For the Jews, empowered with hope and fierce determination, fought back valiantly. No enemy could withstand them, and they won great victories. While they had authority to plunder their enemies, they refrained from doing so, to show that their motive was one of self-defense alone.

Then Xerxes said to Esther, "The Jews have killed and destroyed five hundred men and the ten sons of Haman in the citadel of Susa. What have they done in the rest of the king's provinces? Now what is your petition? It will be given you. What is your request? It will also be granted" (Est. 9:12).

No longer a mere showpiece in the kingdom, Esther would make a strategic military request. Wanting to land a deathblow to the persecution of her people, she asked that they be allowed to defend themselves in Susa for another day and that the bodies of Haman's sons be hung on the gallows as public spectacles. When all was said and done, seventy-five thousand of their enemies throughout the empire had died in the unsuccessful attempt to wipe out the Jews.

What triumphs Esther's daring heart had wrought! What songs of praise must have spilled from her mouth! Her position in the Persian Empire had been strengthened substantially. From then on, she would be a queen whose words carried great authority.

We might see her actions to crush her enemies as excessive vindictiveness on her part. To be sure, she had no mercy on the enemies of God when they came to murder His people. Living on the other side of the cross among pagan people, she didn't understand much about forgiving her enemies. But we should remember that she was forced to contend with wicked and implacable foes who sought the genocide of her race. While we may not commend all of her actions, we still commend her daring heart that risked all for God's people. Not only had God used her to overpower the mighty Haman but also to crush every wicked adversary of His people.

Mordecai made a record of the events and called for an annual two-day celebration of feasting and gift-giving to remember this time when God providentially delivered the Jews from annihilation through Esther's intervention. He and Esther sent letters throughout the kingdom explaining the holiday, which they called Purim (from the word *pur*, meaning "lots," referring to Haman's use of lots for choosing the dates for his massacre of the Jews).

Even today Esther lives on in the hearts of her people the world over as each year Jews celebrate Purim. Customarily, they hold carnival-like celebrations—performing plays and parodies, holding beauty contests, and giving gifts to each other and to the poor. A fast precedes the holiday, the Fast of Esther, commemorating Esther's three days of fasting before approaching the king's throne. Then at the Purim Festival, they commemorate what she did for them. The primary rule related to the joyous occasion is to hear the reading of the book of Esther (one of only two biblical books named for women). Because they hear it each year, most Jews know Esther's story better than any other biblical account. Moreover, whenever persecution has come against the Jewish race, this book has fostered hope for their ultimate deliverance.

Esther is a story for Christians also. The stories of Scripture are our heritage; the promises of Scripture are ours to claim. As God worked in ancient Persia, He still works today on behalf of His people, turning what is meant for evil into good.

Esther rose from a humble orphan to become queen of a vast empire. Brave and lovely, Esther stands for all time as one who, with daring heart, risked everything to save her people—and God's.

Almost thirty years after Esther's heroic acts, King Xerxes' son, Artaxerxes, would send Nehemiah from Susa to rebuild Jerusalem's walls (see Neh. 1:1ff.). How could it have happened without Esther? She saved the Jewish people! Without her there might never have been a Nehemiah or an Ezra. She could not know the full ramifications of her daring act, but she had prepared the way for Christ's coming, halting the efforts of one who tried to wipe out King David's line, from which Christ was born. Truly, God had raised Queen Esther up for "such a time as this."

God of love and God of power, Grant us in this burning hour
Grace to ask these gifts of Thee, Daring hearts and spirits free.
GERALD H. KENNEDY

LESSONS FOR OUR OWN HEARTS

What an amazing turn of events! What a miracle of historic proportions! Esther was just a Jewish orphan when taken into a pagan king's harem. But, oh, what earthshaking things were wrought through her daring heart!

Have you ever stepped out and done something really daring for God? I well remember one of my early experiences. I was so shy that I always flunked my "dialogues" in high school Spanish. I studied frantically, but each time I had to recite something before the class, my mind froze. In college I took a speech class. During my speeches, I shook uncontrollably. After an entire semester of this, I gave my final speech. Had I learned *anything*? Filled with fear and anguish, I squeaked out incoherent words. I saw my professor sitting in the back, shaking her head as if to say, "She's hopeless!"

Then I became a Christian. While my fears didn't change much, I had a passionate desire to share my faith with others. One evening at church I was asked to give a little report about a conference I had attended. There were about thirty people, but it seemed like thirty thousand to me. Trembling wildly as I tried to speak, it was all I could do to keep from tipping over and crashing to the floor.

A few weeks later, Clay went through his "ordination council" to become an ordained minister. The ministers there liked his testimony, and one invited Clay—and his wife—to come speak at his church on a Sunday morning. We just had to give short testimonies. The opportunity excited me because I loved what God had done in my life and wanted to share it. Once I heard the details, however, I almost fainted. The church, First Baptist Church of Redlands (California), had about six hundred people regularly on Sunday mornings, many of whom were retired university professors and pastors. I changed my mind immediately. This was something that I simply could not do!

But I want to! But I can't! But I want to! But I can't! The issue would not die. It was such an incredible opportunity, such a tremendous honor—how could I refuse? But what if I made a complete fool of myself? Back and forth I vacillated. Finally the night before the big event, I told Clay, "I'm going to go in faith and try my best." I had recently listened to a tape by a young woman named Ann Kiemel and heard her say, "Faith is like jumping out of an airplane and trusting that God won't let you go splat." I felt that I had to take the leap.

The next morning, with daring heart, I left with Clay for our mission. I thought I would sit in the congregation, and the pastor would call us up. Clay could give his testimony, and, depending on my level of nervousness, I could say a few words. As the service began, however, the pastor led us through a side door and walked us directly onto the pulpit platform, which seemed like it was elevated twenty-five feet above the packed sanctuary. I nearly died as we seated ourselves on lofty pulpit thrones.

That's when I knew I had made a dreadful error in judgment. I had stupidly courted disaster! Looking down that very long center aisle toward the back, I foresaw paramedics running toward the altar bearing a stretcher to retrieve my body. The service would be ruined. Still, it might provide an unforgettable recessional.

The wait seemed enormous. I grabbed Clay's arm. Feeling my ice-cold grip, he met my wild eyes with worried eyes. I just knew this would end in disaster for him, too, since I was to go first. I heard none of the music, none of the announcements, nothing at all. Then I heard my name. I wasn't risking death like Esther, but I sure thought I was! I knew I would die of fright, but it was too late to turn back. I shakily stood to my feet, tottered over to the immense pulpit, and threw my entire life into God's hands: "If I perish, I perish."

But God had an incredible surprise for me. As I entered that pulpit and opened my mouth, He took over. Suddenly complete peace, heavenly peace—"the peace of God, which transcends all understanding"—fell over me. I began to talk and talk . . . and talk. Poor Clay. I nearly stole all his time without even knowing it! Afterward people came up to the altar, asking me to pray for them, telling me how my words had blessed them. But who was the most blessed of all? You bet. That experience *still* blesses me! For the rest of my life I can recall the first time I took a crazy leap of faith, saw nothing but ground rushing up at me, and God did not let me go splat!

Sometimes the greatest risks we take receive the greatest rewards. I know we must guard against presumption and endeavor never to tempt the Lord by our foolishness, but sometimes it's hard to tell whether God is calling us to faith or if it's just our own presumption. I took the leap that day and learned that a faithful God was with me.

Mine is just a small story of daring to step out on the wings of faith for God. But just think of Esther's courageous act. I merely conquered my own personal demons of fear, but Esther faced off with the Hitler of her time to save her race from genocide. God had planned to save His people all along, and it meant relying on this lovely young woman. She looked soft and innocuous on the outside, but she was destined to be God's instrument, His secret weapon to fell giants. In responding to His call, she had to trade her dainty heart for a daring one and step out boldly into uncharted waters.

How the Lord needs Esthers to rise up and show this type of courage today. The Lord wants us to respond to His call with daring hearts. How can we gain the victories of a daring heart? Here are some key ingredients.

Accept the Challenge

God may not call us to save an entire people or nation. On the other hand, maybe He will! He has set us where we are in history for a reason. He has given us gifts, abilities, opportunities, and challenges for this hour. Whoever and wherever you are, He wants you to accept your duty. He wants you to hear Mordecai's plea: "And who knows but that you have come to royal position for such a time as this?" (4:14). He wants your faint heart replaced with a daring one.

The first obstacles Esther had to conquer were her excuses. When God came calling for her, she probably could have thought of a number of reasons to do nothing. She had suffered enough pain in life. She had lost her parents, had been raised by her relative, was forced from her Jewish home and world, was enslaved in a pagan harem to be used as a sex object. But God had wiped away her tears and raised her to the position of queen. It would have been tempting to rest on her laurels forever. But now this! God wanted her to risk all the security she had won.

But wait! Women—including the queen—were expected to serve their families quietly and compliantly, staying on the fringe of religious and political life. Could God really call her to break through the cultural norms, step outside her confines, and risk her life to do His will? The answer was yes.

But wait again! She had always respected authority, submitting to every requirement. Would God really call her to defy the law of the land—and suffer the consequences? The answer was yes.

Like Esther, we live in a critical hour in history. What risks are you taking for God's kingdom? What are the hindrances to accepting His call? You can look at the challenges and cry, "Why me?" But God knows what you can handle. He puts His resources at your disposal. He may not have chosen you to be a queen, but you are a daughter of God, an even more influential position. Perhaps He has allowed you to bear certain problems and concerns because He trusts you to rise to the occasion. He knows you will, with daring heart, take your stand for Him.

Esther might have thought that God had let her ascend to her high pedestal for her own delight, but soon she learned the true purpose. She had been confined to her palace sanctum, not seeing the big picture. She needed to step outside her narrow confines to see her destiny in the kingdom. God gave her a revelation, calling her to put the interests of His kingdom and His people first. She had to count the cost—her life or her people's, her will or God's. When it came down to it, she made the noble choice. She dared to obey God's call. If God would save her life, then good. If not, then so be it. She placed her life entirely in His hands.

Our goal in life is not to prosper but to be faithful and fruitful for Christ. Those who cling to people, possessions, positions, and life itself, hoping to find security in them, can never have daring hearts for God and can never make a difference in their world. Like Esther, God calls us to put the interests of His kingdom and His people first.

How many of us are hiding out, caught in a flurry of busy activity, letting the world pass by as it hastens on its way to hell? We are afraid; we play it safe. We agree that when it comes to battles, it's a man's world. How we need godly women to rise up today, women who refuse to run or hide, who don't despair, who don't sit back and wait for God or someone else to do their task for them. How we need women who stand up and risk it all for their people, their nation, and their God.

In a world full of crying needs, unparalleled opportunities abound for serving God. Look! They are all around you. Our national life begs for God's people to bring their light and wisdom into the public arena as never before. We have recently suffered great national traumas. The world stands in the balance. You are God's solution. He has a call on your life. Will you renounce self for the sake of God's kingdom and for the good of others? You need not be a queen—just a servant with a daring heart for God. Be faithful where you are, and you'll see ever greater opportunities unfold before you. He placed you in a strategic position "for such a time as this." Can you say in these last days, "If I perish, I perish"? He is worthy of such a sacrifice!

Let goods and kindred go, this mortal life also . . .

MARTIN LUTHER

Prepare for the Challenge

There is a difference between being foolhardy and daring. Two years ago I injured myself water-skiing and this year I got hurt riding a moped. I didn't know how to do either. I was foolhardy—not daring.

The Lord would use us to play a decisive role in thwarting the enemy's evil plans in our world, but we should be cautious. Stepping into enemy territory to serve God involves risk, and we need the power and guidance of the Holy Spirit. It may seem hard to wait, but if we just tear out recklessly with our own plans, heedless of God's plan, we can endanger ourselves. Esther knew about waiting and preparing. She had spent a year of preparation before she was ushered into the palace as queen. But then she needed to prepare for her life's greatest challenge, an extremely dangerous mission.

How did she prepare? First, she called the people to fast and pray. Next, she prepared her own heart, seeking God for the resources she needed for keeping her commitment. A daring heart does not mean a fearless heart. Even the military leader Joshua had been told repeatedly not to fear. How much more did this delicate woman feel fear as she contemplated facing the king and his executioners with her request. In herself she felt powerless. She knew she needed God. Her call for fasting was an admission that it would take more than a daring heart to change things. She needed to know that God was by her side. With His strength, she could courageously push past her fears and stand in His power. She could stand in the face of death and keep on proclaiming, "If I perish, I perish."

Not only did Esther take adequate time to prepare herself spiritually, but she took time to plan her strategy. She went to work gathering facts. God had given her a strategy to become the queen in the first place. With His help, she would prove to be a skilled tactician again. It looked like the devil had won a giant victory. The situation for God's people seemed hopeless. But behind the scenes, God had a secret plan He was unfolding to Esther, one that would bring incredible triumph. She had no guarantees at the time, and she knew that even with the best strategy, she still might die. But she would be prepared.

How would you feel if God called you to do something that carried with it a strong possibility of losing your life? Are you prepared? Are you preparing? Jesus came to destroy the works of the devil (1 John 3:8), but He had to sacrifice Himself. Esther entered enemy territory prepared to sacrifice herself, too. Many believers around the world are paying the ultimate sacrifice for their faith.

Are you willing to be sent into the devil's fortresses? Are you willing to demolish his strongholds (2 Cor. 10:4)? You will need to know his schemes (2 Cor. 2:11). You will need to understand God's resources (1 Cor. 2:12; Eph. 1:18-19). Will you prepare yourself to heed God's call? Ultimately your victory is assured. Either in this life or in the next, you will see your enemy sink before you in wretched defeat as Esther did.

Meet the Challenge

Esther came to know why God gave her the throne. Yet her test of faith could not have come at a worse time. She was sitting under a cloud, feeling neglected, wondering why the king had not called for her in a month. Had she displeased him? Had he lost interest in her? But the circumstances were perfect for God to do what he wanted in Esther's heart. She would never know the victory of a daring heart without these circumstances. She had been kept out of the king's presence so that her heart might become stronger. If the task were easy and carried no risk, she would not have needed a daring heart. If she abandoned her people now, it would mean living with a sick, cowardly, guilty heart for the rest of her life. The only choice for Esther was to rally her inner resources, go into a place that was off-limits to her, and engage the enemy.

Esther did the hard thing. Did the fear Esther felt as she entered the throne room mean that she was in the wrong place at the wrong time? Not at all. She may not have felt God's Spirit upon her life. She may not have felt confident, equipped, or powerful. But she would not let her emotions rule the day. With daring heart she pushed through her fears into God's miracle. Yes, God gives miraculous power to daring hearts *as* they need it. His anointing comes *as* they move in faith and obedience. When we are in earnest about serving Christ, when we release the reins, surrender our all, and step out in faith, there is no telling the wonders God will do in and through us.

Miracle upon miracle unfolded as Esther began her journey of faith and obedience. God anointed her with amazing wisdom, discretion, and grace as He led her through the unfolding drama. It did not take Esther long to recognize God's strong and sovereign hand over the entire affair. She had feared an earthly sovereign, but on her side was the Sovereign of the universe.

As a young woman, Esther was dragged from her simple home to the king's harem. But God was the one who put her in her position ahead of a sinister plan to annihilate the Jewish race. Who would think that God would destine a Jewish exile, orphan, and captive to be the queen of an empire? Who would think God would choose her to save her people?

We should have a sense of destiny that says, "I was created for such a time as this!" (see Esther 4:14). We, too, are placed where He wants us for His purposes. There are no coincidences. When we look at our situations as God-directed, we can more readily cooperate with His purposes and fulfill His plan. God is always working, often patiently and quietly arranging circumstances to bring about His sovereign plan in our lives. If God is moving you into a new situation, and His purpose makes no sense to you, He just may be placing you there for some special reason you cannot yet see.

We had previously suffered and been insulted in Philippi, as you know, but with the help of our God we dared *to tell you his gospel in spite of strong opposition.*

1 THESSALONIANS 2:2, EMPHASIS MINE

You may be in a frightening time in your life where God is calling you to step out in faith and take risks. You can, with daring heart, act courageously in fearsome situations because God is in control. If you rest in His unchanging nature, you can face life's greatest challenges. He can save you from the evils of this world; He can rescue you from the plots of wicked people; He can deliver you from sin and death. You can know with certainty that the God who controls the universe can take care of you, too.

Haman was the king's powerful favorite. We might look at the wicked Hamans of this world and feel quite helpless and hopeless, especially when we see others around us bowing down to them in obeisance. With God on our side, however, these Hamans will be felled. God may never call on you to save an entire people, but of this you can be sure: He has some purpose, some mission, for us all, especially in this momentous time in history when the church might be positioned to enter her finest hour. You and I are here for such a time as this!

In God's Control

Young Esther seemed far from queen material—a lowly Jewish orphan girl in a vast foreign empire, taken into a king's harem. Once she became the queen of this ruthless pagan king, she seemed an unlikely candidate to have a voice in kingdom affairs or to heroically save her people from destruction. But God saw in her a daring heart waiting for its release. He had an anointing for her to discover and walk in. But she had to be pushed to the wall to discover it. Her crisis brought the release her heart needed.

With daring heart she stepped out in faith to right the wrongs done to her people. Pushing her way through the barriers, she approached the king's forbidden throne. When he extended his scepter to her, she dared more. When Haman's scheme was exposed and he was executed, she dared more. When the king would give her anything, and Mordecai became the empire's second-in-command, she dared more. When an irrevocable decree was shoved aside, and Jews throughout the empire rejoiced, she dared more. When the appointed day of the Jewish race's destruction came, and she saw their enemies destroyed, she dared more. Finally when the enemies of her people had been mopped up, and when all seeds of violence and persecution had been uprooted, and when she saw that powerful empire kneel before her, only then did she dare to cease her triumphant campaign. Then she celebrated!

It seemed at first that God was not involved in this story, that He was nowhere to be found, and that He had completely abandoned His people in their dark and devastating hour. We can't even find His name in the entire book! But just as His name is hidden from view, so His work was hidden from view—that is, until the right time. Soon we discover His fingerprints everywhere. As it turns out, no other book of the Bible better illustrates God's sovereign intervention. He was there raising Esther up, allowing Mordecai to uncover a plot, giving the king insomnia, having servants read about Mordecai, sending Esther on a daring mission, bringing a joyful conclusion.

We have a God who controls history. He reigns with absolute sovereignty. No matter how hopeless things might seem or how much we would like to give up, God is in control and can quickly turn things around. Haman was powerful, but He had no knowledge of the God he was up against. When Haman fell, it happened so quickly that he didn't know what hit him. What hope this should give us that God is at work, moving people, conditions, and events in our lives to bring about His purposes and our vindication.

If you believe this—that God is bringing about His perfect plan in a perfect way with perfect timing—you will find yourself able to face life with a daring heart. You will step out in faith, cognizant of your own weakness and vulnerability, but confident of His all-sufficient grace and power to meet your difficult challenge. You will have hope and faith in difficult, dark, and dangerous times. You will have courage to press on to see the enemy's work completely defeated in your life. You will persist in your fight to see your family, your church, and your world revolutionized for God's glory.

God wants to use you powerfully. You are needed and valuable to Him. Be open and available. Allow Him to accomplish His purposes in you. He may use you to accomplish things that others would never consider, things that are greater than you ever would have imagined, even preventing the wholesale ruin of your people, even saving your nation!

Woman of God, the Lord would say to you, "Arise! I will give you a daring heart. I will lay an incredible anointing on you if you step out in faith for Me. You will see miracles. You will rejoice. You will know with certainty that 'for such a time as this' I have placed you here."

With daring hearts for God, powerful kingdoms and wicked rulers can fall beneath us. The Lord calls, "Ask of me, and I will make the nations your inheritance, the ends of the earth your possession" (Ps. 2:8).

Heart Check

1. Has God called you to something that you fear? Are you now ready and willing to be daring for God?

2. How can you prepare for this challenge?

3. Do you have any Hamans in your life? Look up Psalm 37:12-13, 2 Corinthians 1:10, and Romans 8:28. How do these encourage you?

4. Are you able to trust God's sovereignty? How can you better find your security in Him?

5. Compose a prayer to God in response to this chapter's lessons.

6

THE LIBERATED HEART

ACTS 18:1-3, 18-19, 24-28; ROMANS 16:3-5;
1 CORINTHIANS 16:19; 2 TIMOTHY 4:19

MANY IN EPHESUS had heard that a young, popular, and powerful preacher named Apollos had arrived from Alexandria, Egypt—a city famous for its grand libraries and great university. People had flocked to hear him, and he did not disappoint them. Full of passion and conviction, he spoke with great eloquence and persuasiveness. As a talented and enthusiastic young Jewish scholar trained in that Greek learning center, he had been privileged to observe the best orators in the world. He had learned something from them all. He had wanted to be like them, stirring the masses with his brilliantly delivered discourses, roundly silencing those who might oppose him in debate. Indeed, his preaching had stirred everyone.

One couple in the crowd, however, went to talk to the new evangelist. This couple, Aquila and Priscilla (also called Prisca), had responded differently from the others. They were polite enough, but they had not hung on his words. They seemed to think they knew something that he did not, and he had the strangest feeling that they really *did*. But how could they? They were just simple working-class people. What could they tell *him*? Still, something in their eyes and in their spirits—a humble certainty—told him he must listen to them.

He accepted their invitation to go home and share a meal with them. Now he sat in their home, listening intently. Since Jewish women didn't generally teach men, Priscilla amazed him. She didn't just hover in the background, waiting on the men. She took initiative in their conversation. That she possessed deep knowledge of Christian truth was clear to him.

"Your passion for Christ is obvious," she had said, smiling warmly. "But would you like to know the life in Christ more fully?" For all his brilliance and eloquence, he had a serious lack in his understanding, and she knew it. How artfully—with great humility, tact, wisdom, and love—she let him know it, too. He had argued with the greatest men, but this humble Jewish woman easily held her own with him.

As Priscilla, along with Aquila, carefully unfolded the Christian Gospel in its fullness to Apollos, his eyes opened to its full reality. He had always thought there was more. Now he realized he had never heard the whole message of Jesus Christ, and his heart burned within him. As they instructed him and prayed for him, the final pieces of the puzzle came together for a perfect fit, and he was filled with joy.

For Priscilla to so instruct this erudite young preacher showed amazing understanding and confidence on her part. Women were not even allowed to enter discussions with the men in synagogues. But she was passionate for the Lord, filled with His Spirit, and eager to serve Him. So she did—but not defiantly. Christ had qualified her as a minister of His Gospel, and with her husband, she walked in His anointing.

We call Priscilla's heart The Liberated Heart. In an age when women were not outwardly liberated, she never lacked for ways to express her faith. She carried on no rebellious crusade for equality, but she did walk through every door open to her. Working within the confines of her culture, she served the Lord faithfully with wisdom, grace, and maturity, bearing much fruit for Him. Becoming a female leader in a man's world, she rose to a place of incredible prominence in the early church.

What we know of Priscilla and Aquila begins about A.D. 49 in the Grecian city of Corinth. The couple, evidently childless, had recently come from Rome where Emperor Claudius Caesar reigned. After succeeding Caligula, a ruthless megalomaniac, Claudius had done much to stabilize Rome. Generally, he treated the large Jewish colony there with great tolerance. But now, about midway through his reign, he expelled the entire Jewish community from Rome, Christians included. The Roman historian Suetonius, who lived about fifty years later, alludes to this decree, suggesting that the preaching of Christ had caused ongoing disturbances between Christian and non-Christian Jews in the capital city. Claudius was nervous, and, fearing riots, he banished all the Jews, including the Christians, who were considered a Jewish sect.

Since neither Paul nor Luke mentions this couple's conversion, they were likely members of a Christian faction in their synagogue in Rome. Possibly they were converted to Christ during the unrest, or they may have participated in the ministry that led to the ouster of all Jews. What we know for certain is that Aquila had emigrated from Pontus in Asia Minor to Rome, that their life in Rome ended abruptly for them, and that they landed in Corinth. In a time when most people lived and died where they were born, these two would uproot themselves many times.

These were dangerous times. Forced from Rome, they must have prayed hard for the Lord's direction before settling in Corinth. This city gave them ample opportunities for establishing both their business and their ministry. Aquila was a tent-maker, and Priscilla worked alongside him. Fortunately, tent-making was in high demand, so they easily set up their shop in the Corinthian market district to support themselves while they served Christ in ministry.

At that time Corinth was a leading city, not only of Greece (Achaia), but of the world. It was the highly affluent political and commercial center of Greece, even more prominent than Athens. The Isthmian Games (second only to the Olympics) were held here, and the city was situated within easy access of all parts of the Roman Empire. The city was called "the Bridge of Greece," for all north and south traffic in the country had to pass through it. Travelers from every land thronged its streets for business—and for pleasure. Dominating the city's landscape was the hillside Acropolis, which boasted a magnificent temple of the goddess of love and beauty, Aphrodite (Venus). One thousand "sacred" female priests from the temple engaged in religious prostitution with both locals and foreigners. Corinthians had an unrivaled reputation for gross immorality, even among the pagans. With a large mixed population of Romans, Greeks, and Jews, it was a strategic place for Christian missionaries.

Little did Priscilla and Aquila know that when God sent them to Corinth, He had a special mission in mind for them. He had someone for them to meet, a Christian missionary who needed their help. One day Aquila came in the door with a tired and serious-looking stranger. "Priscilla, let me introduce you to someone I met today," said Aquila.

Priscilla always enjoyed having guests, and she greeted this one warmly. She didn't know that this visitor would change her life forever—that this man was unlike anyone she ever had met or ever would meet again. In fact, this man and this couple would become lifelong friends and coworkers, and their partnership in the Gospel of Christ would leave a profound mark in world history.

"Your name?" she asked.

"I'm Paul, an apostle of the Lord Jesus Christ," came the reply.

"He's a preacher of the Good News and travels from city to city," explained Aquila, "and he's just come to Corinth from Athens. You should hear the stories he's been telling me!"

"I'm eager to hear them," she said. "Please join us for supper." Sensitive to the Holy Spirit and to the needs of others, she added, "Stay the night with us if you count us worthy."

What relief swept over Paul. When they met him that day,

Priscilla and Aquila had no idea of the extent of his need. He was on his second missionary journey (A.D. 50-52) and had just come to town in low spirits. In Philippi he had been beaten severely and thrown in prison (Acts 16:22-24). In Thessalonica, after riots, friends had to smuggle him out of town by night (17:10). In Berea disturbances led him to flee from the region (17:14). In Athens, his first outreach to Greece, he became emotionally distressed before preaching at the Areopagus. While he made some converts there, his ministry was largely unsuccessful, and no church would spring from it (17:16, 32-34).

Now he had come to the second great Greek city, exhausted, discouraged, broke, and overwhelmed. Add to all this his feeling of loneliness. He was used to traveling in teams, but in his trouble at Berea, he had gotten separated from his companions, Silas and Timothy. He'd hoped they would rejoin him in Athens, but they had not come. So he went on to Corinth alone but in no condition for the challenges there. By his own admission, he came to Corinth with misgivings: "I came to you in weakness and fear, and with much trembling" (1 Cor. 2:3). Perhaps he was even suffering from an illness.

With no friends or support, Paul needed help and encouragement. He also needed to find a way to support himself. He no doubt prayed, "Where do I go from here, Lord? I'm so exhausted." But God had already provided for him. Wandering through the marketplace, looking for someone to hire on with, he bumped into Aquila. Little did he know that he would find in this man and his wife bosom friends with hearts for ministry after his own. One of his greatest missions would take place in Corinth, due in part to their commitment to stand with him.

Paul had a four-ply bond with his new friends: They were Jews by birth, Christians by faith, tent-makers by trade, and missionaries at heart. Much to Paul's delight, they invited him to move in with them and to work with them in their tent-making business for as long as he liked. Throughout his ministry, none would care and provide for Paul as would Priscilla and Aquila. With their loving support, it did not take long for his strength to revive.

What mutual joy these three brought to each other. With their common passion for Christ, they must have enjoyed wonderful times together in fellowship, prayer, and worship, and in discussing the Scriptures. What exceptional teaching, what marvelous theological training Priscilla and Aquila must have received from the apostle Paul, the Early Church's greatest gospel expositor. And what marvelous training they got from his example and experience. Paul shared with them his wealth of spiritual wisdom, and they shared with him their love, support, and partnership.

Priscilla and Aquila had no trouble entering wholeheartedly into Paul's ministry. The three went to synagogue together every Sabbath, where he reasoned with both Jews and Greeks, trying to convince them of the Gospel's claims. The couple listened eagerly to his messages, praying for him, encouraging him, ready to lay down their lives for the ministry.

Finally Silas and Timothy arrived from Macedonia, and Paul ceased his work of making tents and gave himself exclusively to preaching. With Priscilla and Aquila's gift of hospitality, they probably supported the entire ministry team, and their home became a center for fellowship.

Women could not speak in the Jewish synagogues, but they found freedom of expression in their homes. In a house church men and women were not segregated but worshiped and learned together. This freed a woman like Priscilla to exercise her ministry gifts. At the same time, she never threatened the men in her life. We don't detect rivalry with her husband or with Paul or with any other men in the church. They obviously were happy to recognize and affirm her gifts.

As in previous cities, opposition did arise against Paul's ministry, and Jews became abusive toward him. Shaking out his clothes in protest against them, Paul left the synagogue, saying that from then on he would preach to the Gentiles. Priscilla and Aquila no doubt supported him in this decision and went with him. He must have felt some insecurity though, because one night the Lord spoke to him in a vision, saying, "Do not be afraid; keep on speaking, do not be silent. For I am with you, and no one is going to attack and harm you, because I have many people in this city" (Acts 18:9-10).

Despite other incidents with the Jews, Paul stayed on for a year and a half with Priscilla and Aquila, teaching and preaching. They always knew Paul would eventually move on, and one day he approached them with the news that he was heading for Syria. But after living together all this time, they were now solid family—so solid, in fact, that he wanted them to join him. The church was firmly established in Corinth, and the couple had missionary hearts, too. Delighted to share in Paul's mission, they packed up a few things and headed out to assist him.

Sailing straight across the Aegean Sea, they came to Ephesus (in Asia). After several days, the three agreed that Paul would sail back to Antioch while Priscilla and Aquila would stay until he returned. Why did they stay? Perhaps the Ephesians wanted Paul to spend more time with them, but feeling pressed to move on, he left Priscilla and Aquila there in his stead. He knew they were fully capable of sharing Christ with the Ephesians and discipling them.

It would prove to be a decision with God's fingerprints all over it. Priscilla and Aquila would stay busy with tent-making, and again their home became a meeting place. But also God had a very specific divine appointment for them. Continuing with Paul's example of sharing the Gospel first with the Jews before going to the Gentiles, they frequented the local synagogue.

One day at the synagogue, the eloquent young scholar, apologist, and debater from Alexandria entered Ephesus and church history. Apollos was a believer who spoke fervently about Jesus. He was well educated, with a thorough knowledge of the Scriptures. Having read, studied, memorized, lived, breathed, and preached them, he was even considered "mighty in the Scriptures" (Acts 18:24 KJV). With all his talent and passion, he debated opponents of Christianity forcefully, persuasively, and fearlessly.

So Aquila and Priscilla heard Apollos speak that day and were impressed with him. They appreciated his sincerity, his passion, and his gifts. He was inflamed with zeal for God's glory and Christ's honor, and he preached as faithfully, diligently, and accurately as he knew how. Yet they spotted the holes in his theology. For all his impressiveness, he still did not know the Word as well as this simple couple who had been trained under the apostle Paul.

What flaw did they notice? They detected that Apollos did not know the whole gospel story but had heard and believed only a portion of the Christian message. His preaching was based on the Old Testament and John the Baptist's message. He only knew "the baptism of John"—a confession of sin and repentance. John had pointed to Christ, and through him Apollos knew the call to repent and follow Jesus. He recognized Jesus as the Messiah, but he knew nothing of the good news of salvation through the cross of Christ. Neither did he know of the coming of the Holy Spirit in power. Christ was his hero but not his Savior.

Priscilla knew exactly where Apollos's message fell short and was discerning enough to recognize that his limited knowledge might damage the cause of Christ. She could have criticized him behind his back or looked the other way, choosing not to interfere in hopes that someone else would do it. But she didn't. While some might have confronted him publicly in the synagogue or outside in front of others, she would not, even if she could.

If she cringed at the sermon she had just heard, she refused to show it. She saw Apollos's heart for God. This passionate young man, if properly taught, could be a powerful instrument for spreading Christ's Gospel in the world. Wanting to win him to full faith, she would in no way lay a stumbling block for him.

Priscilla was hospitable, especially to itinerant preachers. She and Aquila knew what to do. After introducing themselves, they warmly invited Apollos home with them. In the privacy of their home, they could share very openly and personally with him the full message of Christ.

Priscilla was one of those amazing women who seems to have time to do everything. Not only did she work at the family business, keep her house, and still have time for guests, but she also was an avid student of the Word of God, and she learned the Gospel of Jesus Christ thoroughly. Women were not allowed to teach publicly in Roman or Jewish culture. But they could communicate in private. As she would prove, she could do more than just share her ideas. Spiritually gifted in areas of wisdom and leadership, she could teach and correct the eloquent young man with great eloquence herself.

She and Aquila befriended Apollos. They didn't criticize him, but with gentleness, grace, and humility led him to a fuller understanding of the truth. With their differences in age, occupation, education, ethnicity, and gender, Priscilla must have impressed him greatly for him to listen to her. Her spiritual insight and experience must have astonished him. Correcting the teaching of a dynamic male evangelist and teacher would seem off-limits to most women. But Priscilla communicated straightforwardly, unashamedly, and effectively, proving to him that there was more to believing in Jesus as the Messiah than following John's baptism.

Such was Priscilla's own persuasiveness that she persuaded this powerfully persuasive man. Scripture after Scripture that he had preached became clearer to him. Now he understood! This divine encounter would change the entire scope of Apollos's life and ministry. When he left their presence that day, he had the complete Gospel. Now he knew Jesus as more than a historic hero who died and who provided an example to follow; he knew Jesus as a living presence. Watch out, world! He had been enthusiastic before, but now, filled with assurance of salvation and with the Holy Spirit's fire, his effectiveness as a preacher must have increased a thousandfold.

Priscilla and Aquila would multiply their ministry many times over in Apollos alone as he began to pass on what he had learned from them. He traveled on to Achaia (Greece) for the important work God had prepared for him there. He carried with him a letter of recommendation from the Ephesian leaders, likely composed by Priscilla and Aquila. Their endorsement would be important since they had been prominent in the fellowship at Corinth, located in Achaia.

A powerful instrument in God's hand, Apollos immediately caused a sensation. He became the verbal champion of the believers in the region, vigorously refuting Jewish opponents in public debates. Powerfully proving by the Scriptures that Jesus was the Christ, he silenced them. God used him mightily to strengthen and encourage the church and to convince many others of the truth of the Gospel.

Through no fault of his own, a dedicated following arose there in Corinth. These believers saw Apollos as their apostle, even putting him before Paul and Peter. In their spiritual immaturity, the church split into factions. In Paul's letter to the Corinthians, he corrected this factionalism, saying, "For when one says, 'I follow Paul,' and another, 'I follow Apollos,' are you not mere men? What, after all, is Apollos? And what is Paul? Only servants, through whom you came to believe—as the Lord has assigned to each his task. I planted the seed, Apollos watered it, but God made it grow" (1 Cor. 3:4-6).

We can only imagine the hot debates as church leaders struggled over their loyalties. Paul and Apollos were both mighty men of God who had made great contributions to the church of Corinth. But so had Priscilla. She had preceded both men to Corinth. She had opened the door to Paul and stood beside him in his efforts to plant the seed there. She had instructed Apollos, preparing him for his ministry of watering the seed. Through Priscilla's effort, the early church received in Apollos a preacher second only to Paul in influence. Some think Apollos authored the book of Hebrews. If so, just think of the importance of Priscilla's and Aquila's early instruction to him. What he had become, he owed to their contribution. Paul could write to the Corinthian church, "I always thank God for you because of his grace given you in Christ Jesus" (1 Cor. 1:4). This is a tribute, in part, to Priscilla's work among them.

Surely Paul and Apollos both would recognize Priscilla's key role in their success. She stood alongside them as their dedicated partner in the Gospel. She was a woman in a culture that did not fully appreciate women. Nevertheless, with her liberated heart, God used her mightily.

While Apollos ministered in Corinth, Paul rejoined Priscilla and Aquila in Ephesus. The apostle spoke boldly and persuasively for Christ in the synagogue. Within a few months, however, he was so frustrated with the obstinate Jews there that he left, taking the other believers with him. They met daily instead in a local lecture hall.

This was an intense and fruitful time for the ministry team. Paul did extraordinary miracles there in Ephesus. The sick were healed, and demons were cast out. When the sons of Sceva were routed by demons they tried to cast out, people all over Ephesus were seized with fear and held the Christian faith in high honor. People repented of their occult practices, and they destroyed their materials in a multimillion dollar bonfire (in today's currency). So intense was this time of ministry that within two years every Jew and Greek in the entire province had heard the Gospel!

All the while Priscilla and Aquila kept using their home for the Lord. The church regularly gathered there for fellowship, training, and worship. Near the end of Paul's ministry in Ephesus (A.D. 55), he wrote his first letter to the Corinthians, possibly from their home. He wanted to visit Corinth again, but he informed them, "I will stay on at Ephesus until Pentecost, because a great door for effective work has opened to me, and there are many who oppose me" (1 Cor. 16:8-9).

Paul also tacked onto his letter a special greeting: "The churches in the province of Asia send you greetings. Aquila and Priscilla greet you warmly in the Lord, and so does the church that meets at their house" (1 Cor. 16:19). What great love for God's people, what undying passion for Christ Priscilla and Aquila possessed!

At this time Paul became concerned for the mother church in Jerusalem. The disciples there were in poverty, having been cut off from their Jewish families, jobs, and community because of their allegiance to Jesus. And now a famine had hit. Paul intended to swing through Macedonia (which included churches in Philippi, Thessalonica, and Berea) and Achaia (which included the church in Corinth). While strengthening these churches, he would also collect offerings for the Jerusalem church. From there he would go on to Jerusalem, offerings in hand.

Preparing to leave Ephesus for this trip, he sent team members Timothy and Erastus on ahead to Macedonia. But before he could leave, trouble broke out in Ephesus related to the goddess Artemis (Diana). The Ephesians put great faith in her. She was a fertility goddess who, they believed, nurtured all living beings. Her magnificent temple in Ephesus was considered the fourth of the Seven Wonders of the Ancient World. The Gospel was damaging business for those who made shrines and silver idols for worshiping the goddess, and one particular silversmith started a huge riot. The crazed crowd began shrieking, "Great is Artemis of the Ephesians!" and seized two members of Paul's team from Macedonia. In a frenzied rush, they carried them to the local theater (recently excavated, this theater seated thirty thousand). Paul wanted to go to the theater and reason with them. His friends, however, thought better of the idea. They knew this crazed mob was in no mood for debating him. After all, it was his blood they were after!

In one of those rare instances where someone prevailed over Paul, his friends risked their own lives to shuttle him away to safety. Who were these friends? Most likely, Priscilla and Aquila, as we will see.

Paul left Ephesus. This had been an extremely dangerous incident, and perhaps Priscilla and Aquila were still in danger themselves. At any rate, they chose to leave Ephesus at around the same time. The Emperor Claudius had died two years earlier, in A.D. 54, and this had opened the door for Jews to return to Rome. Evidently knowing their ministry was needed there and sensing the Spirit's urging as well, they headed back to their former home in Rome.

Meanwhile Paul arrived in Greece where he stayed for three months. During his time in Corinth, he wrote his epistle to the Romans (A.D. 56). In closing this letter, he sends his personal greetings to his many friends there. Heading the list is Priscilla, followed by Aquila: "Greet Priscilla and Aquila, my fellow workers in Christ Jesus" (Rom. 16:3). What a close bond of friendship they shared. How indebted Paul felt for their faithful partnership in the cause of Christ. Priscilla had been a faithful and effective minister, laboring with Paul in spreading the Gospel and discipling the young church through the good times and the bad. Giving her the ultimate tribute, he praises her as his "fellow worker."

Not only did Paul greet Priscilla and Aquila, but with deep gratitude, he asserts, "They risked their lives for me" (Rom. 16:4). More literally translated, he says, "who for my life their own neck did lay down."[1] In other words, during a time of mortal danger when martyrdom loomed—probably in the Ephesus riot—Priscilla and Aquila laid their necks on the chopping block for Paul. Others might have tried to save their own necks from disaster, but Priscilla had jeopardized hers to save Paul. With her liberated heart, she had not sat timidly by, leaving the matter to the men. Asserting herself, she played a key part in saving the apostle's life, and with it his entire future ministry.

Paul would never forget Priscilla's and Aquila's tremendous sacrifice for him and for the Gospel; nor would all the churches that God had used him to plant. He says, "Not only I but all the churches of the Gentiles are grateful to them" (Rom. 16:4). The Greek word used here for "Gentiles," *ethnos*, is also translated "nations." Just think! All the peoples of all the churches throughout the nations of that time— Italy, Sicily, Macedonia, Achaia, Thrace, Asia, Galatia, Lycia, Pisidia, Syria, etc.—would admire, esteem, and feel deep gratitude toward this one couple.

Finally Paul says, "Greet also the church that meets at their house" (Rom. 16:5). In this time of persecution and poverty, it was neither possible nor safe for the Christians to meet in buildings; so they worshiped together in private homes. Throughout her ministry, Priscilla had sanctified her home for God's purposes. Now back in Rome only a few months, a church was already established in her home. She had left Rome in a persecution, she had experienced persecution since then, and soon the fiercest of persecutions would hit the church in Rome. To triumph in this dreadful hour, the oppressed Christians would desperately need the inspiration and guidance of an anointed woman of God with a liberated heart.

Claudius was gone, but his adopted son, Nero Claudius Caesar (Emperor Nero), succeeded him. At first Nero was a benign ruler, hating even to sign the death sentences of criminals. Within a few years, however, he would be so brutal as to order the deaths of his own mother and his wife. After that he would begin a campaign against Christians so savage that the church would come to view him as the Antichrist.

Soon Paul would be arrested in Jerusalem and then imprisoned in Caesarea for two years. When finally given a trial, he would appeal to Caesar, which would ultimately lead to his transfer to Rome. When he reached Rome, he would await trial under house arrest for another two years. During this time he "welcomed all who came to see him" (Acts 28:30). We can imagine that his dear friends Priscilla and Aquila would visit him often. History is not clear about what happened next with Paul. It is assumed that he was released, did some additional traveling, and then was arrested and imprisoned in Rome a second time.

A terrible fire broke out in Rome in A.D. 64. It raged for six days and seven nights and totally destroyed a great part of the city. It was rumored among the Roman populace that Nero had set the fire so he could rebuild Rome more gloriously. Christians were not well liked because they refused to sacrifice to the Roman gods or participate in holidays or patriotic festivals, most of which involved worship of

Roman gods. Therefore, to remove suspicion from himself, Nero shifted the blame to the Christians and began a savage campaign against them.

A Roman official and historian at the time, Tacitus, reported in his *Annals* concerning Nero: "Hence, to suppress the rumor, he falsely charged with the guilt, and punished with the most exquisite tortures, the persons commonly called Christians. . . ." (*Annals*, xv. 44). He explains that a vast multitude were convicted of hating the human race and were put to death. One torture involved nailing Christians to crosses and burning them as torches for Nero's gardens at night. The more merciful deaths he ordered were at the claws of wild beasts in the arena.

Sometime during this period, perhaps fleeing Rome, Priscilla and Aquila returned to Ephesus, along with Timothy, another of Paul's longtime friends. While Paul was in prison awaiting trial in Rome, he wrote his second letter to Timothy (A.D. 66-67). At this point, with no hope of release, he sensed his end was near. In this sad letter, his last, he mentions many of his former associates, mostly to report their absence or defection. But also he greets a few people: "Greet Priscilla and Aquila and the household of Onesiphorus" (2 Tim. 4:19). Their lifelong friendship must have meant a lot to the lonely man sitting on death row in a Roman prison. How it must have gladdened his heart to remember them. Though separated by distance, he could rest assured his dear friends were with him in spirit, as always.

Paul—called "the Great Lion of God"—was the first important missionary and theologian in Christian history. Like his blessed Lord, he knew what it was to be "despised and rejected . . . acquainted with grief" (Isa. 53:3 KJV). He suffered enough tribulations for a hundred lifetimes (see 2 Cor. 11:23-29). Amid so many extreme circumstances, he had needed encouragement. Yes, the Lord always stood at his side, but he needed human friends, too. Priscilla and Aquila were God's answer for him.

When they first met Paul, a discouraged and lonely missionary in

Corinth, they replenished his heart by their friendship. With undying affection, they would stand by him in the coming years. How many times did they take him home and wash his wounds and pray him through his dilemmas? Some view the churches of Corinth and Ephesus as his most successful ministries. Undoubtedly, Priscilla and Aquila played a significant role in that success. Truly they were partners in ministry par excellence, and Paul held them in the highest esteem. Yes, Paul would find many coworkers along the way, but none would shine more brightly than Priscilla and Aquila.

We know Paul's missionary journeys well, but Priscilla and Aquila became significant missionaries as well. While our information on their movements is sketchy, we see them move from Rome, to Corinth, to Ephesus, again to Rome, and finally back to Ephesus. Through all the changes, adventures, and difficulties, this couple was a team. It's hard to mention one without the other because the Scriptures never do. They were united in experiencing God's saving grace, united in love and zeal for Him, united in service for Him and His church. They were two hearts beating as one, living a concert of love and labor for their Lord. Christ was first; Christ was all—they both agreed.

Yet while Priscilla worked in partnership with her husband, with Paul, and with the church, she stands as a superlative minister in her own right. She proved she could be a full and trusted partner in ministry with the men. She traveled, taught, entertained, helped earn money, and also helped lead churches in various provinces.

Ever faithful to the Lord and His call, we never hear her crying, "Why me?" as she moved time after time. Nor do we hear her crying, "Why not me?" when it came to serving Christ. With her liberated heart, she never worried about what she could not do as a woman. She had plenty to do. Serving boldly, she went anywhere, did anything, paid any price for the cause of Christ. Serving humbly, she never worried about posturing herself for more status. She was no self-proclaimed minister. Unlike Miriam who challenged Moses for a higher position, God let Priscilla rise to prominence naturally, as cream rises to the top.

In the New Testament, we see Priscilla and Aquila directly mentioned six times. In Acts 18:2 Aquila's name precedes that of Priscilla because Paul met him first. In 1 Corinthians 16:19, the earliest reference to the couple (A.D. 55), Aquila's name precedes that of his wife. In the other Scriptures, however, an interesting pattern emerges. Against all social conventions, Paul puts Priscilla's name before Aquila's in his later letters—Romans 16:3 (A.D. 56), 2 Timothy 4:19 (A.D. 66-67). Luke, also writing later, puts her name first in Acts 18:18 and 18:26 (A.D. 63-70).[2]

Some Bible experts believe that as time went on, Priscilla figured more prominently in the Christian community than Aquila. Perhaps her personal attainments were so impressive and she was so dynamic and so helpful that she emerged as the more publicly recognized leader of the two. We can guess that if she outshone or outranked Aquila, it did not bother him. They seemed to be one in heart, and he must have praised the Lord for her ministry. Clearly, she is one of the most influential women in the New Testament. Although she is mentioned a mere six times, these few verses are packed with love, honor, and devotion. Marching victoriously through the fires of ministry and persecution, Priscilla ultimately blessed the world with her faithfulness. In Rome today a church of St. Prisca stands on the site of a very early church. According to legend, Priscilla's house church in Rome occupied this very site.

Shortly after sending his final letter to Timothy, probably that year, Paul would suffer martyrdom in Nero's persecution, as would the apostle Peter. Tradition says that Priscilla and Aquila also joined the ranks of Christian martyrs. The Roman Catholic Martyrology (an official list of martyrs) commemorates them on July 8.

Priscilla and Aquila may have caught each other's eyes one last time before their executions, conveying what was in their hearts—a confidence that said, in the words of their good friend, "[We] have fought the good fight, [we] have finished the race, [we] have kept the faith" (2 Tim. 4:7). Then, with a nod that said, "Farewell, my beloved. We will meet in heaven," they were ushered out of this life into eternal glory to don their martyrs' crowns. Now Priscilla was liberated in the fullest sense—for all eternity.

LESSONS FOR OUR OWN HEARTS

Many years ago, as a young wife and mother, I sat at a conference in the Midwest watching a couple speak at a workshop. I cannot even remember their topic. What I do remember was that the woman seemed so fulfilled, so whole and free, as she shared alongside her husband. As I watched, my heart wailed within me, for I was locked in an authoritarian system that had stolen my own freedom in Christ.

Have you ever seen a doormat with a big smiley face painted on it? Well, that was my image of what God wanted for me. The headship doctrine under which I suffered at that time had so enslaved me that it convinced me that my greatest task in life was to submit—submit to my husband, the elders, the church, and God. When I could let all the authorities in my life trudge over me with a joyful heart and a smile on my face, then I would have attained true maturity—and liberation. Liberation from what? From "self," of course. The devil dangled before me the notion that if I could just die to self, I would experience the true joy of the Lord.

The devil forgot to tell me the big difference between dying to self-centeredness and having your sense of personhood squashed. What I thought would lead to a liberated heart drove me down a cold, dark path into ever-increasing bondage and despair. Of course, I did need to die to self, just as we all do. There is something very healthy about that process. But there was nothing healthy about having my personhood stolen from me. I was broken, but it was not a godly brokenness. It did not bring spiritual maturity; nor did it bring joy, satisfaction, or liberation. It damaged me. My heart lost hope.

God set me (and Clay) free from that enslaving teaching and

structure on my thirtieth birthday. Interestingly enough, many years later at the very spot where I had despairingly watched the happy couple speak, something wonderful happened. Clay and I spoke together there, too. Now I was a woman with a liberated heart!

In Christ's body, "If one part suffers, every part suffers with it; if one part is honored, every part rejoices with it" (1 Cor. 12:26). Try telling that to Tertullian, a prominent Christian theologian of the second century. Before telling women what they should wear, Tertullian said, "And do you not know that you are (each) an Eve? The sentence of God on this sex of yours lives in this age: the guilt must of necessity live too. You are the devil's gateway: you are the unsealer of that (forbidden) tree: you are the first deserter of the divine law: you are she who persuaded him whom the devil was not valiant enough to attack. You destroyed so easily God's image, man. On account of your desert—that is, death—even the Son of God had to die."[3]

Just try to imagine the joy in the hearts of the women who sat under this man's preaching! I am so thankful for a husband and pastor who doesn't treat women like that. I don't think the apostle Paul did either. Yet a woman in my former church hated Paul "because he hates women," she said. She refused even to come to Bible studies related to Paul. Isn't it interesting then that a woman who knew Paul intimately was so dedicated to him that she would risk her very life for him? Perhaps many of us have misunderstood Paul. After all, wasn't he the one who declared that the cross of Christ brings equality to all? Didn't he say that in Christ "there is no longer male and female; for all of you are one in Christ Jesus" (Gal. 3:28 NRSV)?

Maybe the woman in my church wasn't really hearing Paul's heart. Paul honored Priscilla, recognizing the validity of her ministry and the greatness of her contributions. Don't you think that if Paul or her husband, Aquila, had thought it inappropriate for her to participate in instructing a man or coleading a house church that she would have backed off from doing it? But they obviously didn't. She caught the true spirit of Paul and moved in the anointing he affirmed in her. When Paul saw her, he didn't see a woman but a minister.

Priscilla rose to prominence and leadership as she worked alongside the men, but she did so in a humble and submissive spirit. The men would not have respected her had she been angry, rebellious, or self-aggrandizing. Paul clearly had to correct problems within the church that included disorderly women who didn't know how to behave in church. In a culture where generally the only women who spoke publicly were immoral, Paul had a concern not to bring reproach to the Gospel. His writings make clear his desire to avoid putting stumbling blocks in the way of belief in Christ.

Yet Paul welcomed not only Priscilla but other women as well to work with him as leaders. Paul's heart shows no gender bias, only a regard for the honor of Christ and the spread of His Gospel.

Granted, some of Paul's teachings are troubling at first. Look at 1 Timothy 2:11-12, for example. "A woman should learn in *quietness* [Greek, *hesuchia*] and full submission. I do not permit a woman to teach or to have authority over a man; she must be *silent* [Greek, *hesuchia*]" (emphasis mine). But look also at a preceding verse: "I urge, then, first of all, that . . . prayers . . . be made for everyone . . . that we may live peaceful and *quiet* [Greek, *hesuchios*] lives. . . ." (1 Tim. 2:1-2, emphasis mine). The difference between the Greek words *hesuchia* and *hesuchios* is one of gender and part of speech, not essential meaning. If women are to keep silent in 1 Timothy 2:11-12, then, according to verses 1-2, the whole church should always live silent lives in the world. But that can't be what he means. What Paul is really saying in these verses is that we should have peaceful, orderly lives, both in the church and in the world.

I believe in headship. I believe the Scriptures are clear about submission, but submission does not mean subjection or subjugation. That's what the devil does—conquering, subduing, and enslaving people. God, however, does not steal freedom. We yield in submission to Him because He loves us. Submission in the biblical sense is liberating. It is a matter of love, respect, and devotion. The ultimate proof that there is nothing stifling or degrading about it is that Christ, who was God in human flesh, always is submissive to His Father.

Priscilla had a submissive heart toward her husband and toward Paul. I think that was part of her liberation. She knew who she was, and the men accepted her. Walking beside them, she was no second-class member of the team. She was not their slave but their partner, playing a key role in their adventure and in their success.

The issue of the role of women in the church is a controversial one among well-meaning Christians. I will tell you my husband's position. He generally believes—and I agree—that if God gives spiritual gifts to women, then He expects the church to structure itself in a way that releases them to use those gifts. Clay, therefore, has several women on his staff who do excellent jobs. I preached the sermon this past Mother's Day.

All this said though, this chapter is not about how the church should treat us as women so much as about our having liberated hearts. Here are some things we should know about liberated hearts.

No Freedom Without Liberated Hearts

Some good things have come from the women's rights movement. Women now have more freedom and enjoy more opportunities than previously known in our nation's history. Unfortunately, much of our so-called liberation also has driven us into deeper bondage than ever before.

For one example, look at the area of sexual relationships. Charles Colson says, "The sexual revolution promised liberation from traditional morality, but the only folks liberated were men."[4] ABC News (July 26, 2001) cited a study called "Hooking Up, Hanging Out, and Hoping for Mr. Right: College Women on Mating and Dating Today." The study found that 83 percent of college women want to get married. The "hook-up" culture (casual sexual encounters) they embrace, however, militates against their goal of finding a committed marriage partner. Not only do the women inflict immense pain upon themselves, but according to Dr. Drew Pinsky, host of the MTV show *Loveline*, a college campus is a young man's perfect world. For the men, this is a very comfortable situation.

Is this really liberation? College women might think they are liberated and may even boast of their freedom. But they are not free; they are dying inside. How succinctly the proverb puts it: "Sometimes there is a way that seems to be right, but in the end it is the way to death" (Prov. 16:25 NRSV). If we want true liberation in life, it must start at the heart level. The psalmist says, "I run in the path of your commands, *for you have set my heart free*" (Ps. 119:32, emphasis mine). When we have liberated hearts, it is a joy to obey God's standards.

When it comes to true liberation, the world simply cannot deliver on its promises. The god of this world (2 Cor. 4:4) won't let it. He lures people with vain promises of liberation, only to lead them to hell. Jesus, on the other hand, loves us. He sets our hearts free and blesses our lives. Speaking first of the devil and then Himself, He claims, "The thief's purpose is to steal and kill and destroy. My purpose is to give life in all its fullness" (John 10:10 NLT).

Are you looking to the world to meet the needs of your heart? Only in Jesus Christ will you find true satisfaction. Give yourself fully to Him. He wants to liberate your heart and life.

Then you will know the truth, and the truth will set you free.

JOHN 8:32

So if the Son sets you free, you will be free indeed.

JOHN 8:36

Now the Lord is the Spirit, and where the Spirit of the Lord is, there is freedom.

2 CORINTHIANS 3:17

Our Identity in Christ and Freedom

I think the church needs to affirm its women. Yet no matter how the church, society, or anyone else views us, we must see ourselves the way God does—as precious, beloved, qualified, blessed, affirmed. When we have liberated hearts, external circumstances, however oppressive, cannot defeat us. That is why the enemy of our souls tries so hard to plunder our hearts. If he can conquer the heart, he can conquer the whole person. One who is a victim in her heart cannot stay free from victimization externally.

Early in my marriage my mom gave me Christmas money, and I spent it on a lovely dress. I had never spent so much on a dress in my life, but my girlfriend talked me into it. I went home feeling so guilty. As I sheepishly pulled it out of the bag to show Clay, he jumped all over me. "How could you have done that?" he barked.

Finally after letting him browbeat me for a while, something rose within me, and I spouted, "I'm not taking any more of this! I rarely buy myself anything nice, and this was a gift from *my* mother. What right do *you* have to tell me how I can spend my mother's gift? Why are you treating me this way?"

He immediately fell silent and thought about it for a moment. Then he replied meekly, "I don't know. You just seemed to draw it out of me. I'm sorry."

I think Clay had hit the nail right on the head. This was not something he had done to me; this was something I had done to myself. He had just cooperated. I felt guilty, ashamed, undeserving. Letting myself be victimized was a way for me to let Clay help me do penance. It was also a way for me to sink into self-pity over the way he treated me. I could blame him. I'm so glad I stood up to him (and to my own sickness) that day. I learned something about myself (I was my own worst enemy) and something about my husband (he really was on my side). I also learned that Christ had healing for me, but if I wanted a liberated heart, I had to choose it.

Liberated Hearts and Restrictive Barriers

As women, we can feel so small and vulnerable, so useless to God's purposes. The devil can perpetually point to the line in front of us and convince us that we must not step across it. He loves to put limits on what we can do for God. But what happens when we feel a restlessness, a stirring, a sense of calling that we just can't ignore? What do we do when we want to let God use us in some way that crosses the line? We can look to the church, but sometimes the church, which should be a woman's place of support, turns on us. Not only can the church stifle us from using our gifts, but the church can suppress us in the name of Christ. Told that our perceptions are wrong, we can feel guilty and try to stuff them down. This hardly liberates us.

Some women are happy for an excuse to sit on the sidelines and don't seem to mind living under such oppression. When it comes to serving the Lord, they can say, "I'm just a woman. God doesn't expect anything special of me." For the rest of us, however, who don't like living under oppression, who have a sense of purpose and destiny and want our lives to make a difference in the church and the world, we must use our gifts. Paul says in Galatians 5:1, "It is for freedom that Christ has set us free. Stand firm, then, and do not let yourselves be burdened again by a yoke of slavery." That includes God's daughters! If your church seriously curtails your freedom in Christ, it might be time to consider finding another church.

Did Priscilla settle for second class? Did she agree to second best? The Scriptures don't say so. She used her gifts to her fullest ability, and Paul cheered her on. God used her mightily through her ministry in her house church. Nowhere does Luke say in his book of Acts, "Just to clear up any misunderstandings, I want you all to know that Priscilla did not teach Apollos, and she also kept her mouth shut in her home meetings." Nowhere do we hear of Apollos running around to the churches and saying, "I just want to make it clear that Priscilla had absolutely nothing to say to me." Apollos listened to Priscilla. Her teaching, along with Aquila's, changed his life radically.

Priscilla was exceptional because she became a Christian leader who ranked among her male counterparts. She had their respect. She never needed to push herself on the men. With a wonderful humility that enveloped her use of her influence, she just served as God allowed. He did the rest. Just as Deborah shattered stereotypes of women and leadership in her time, so Priscilla did in hers.

My best men are women.

GENERAL WILLIAM BOOTH, SALVATION ARMY[5]

Liberated from Self-centeredness

Here is a dichotomy. Priscilla asserted herself, boldly using her gifts. At the same time, she lived humbly, ever the simple and faithful servant. Someone preoccupied with her own needs and those of her own family gives little thought to others. But Priscilla's passion for the Lord easily extended to a passion for His people. She wanted to see them established in the faith, and people were naturally drawn to her doorstep and to her heart.

In her society she was just a woman. She probably never thought about making a name for herself. Her foremost ambition was to help the work of Christ advance. She was content to labor in the background, making others great. Paul and Apollos, two great men in the early church whom God used mightily to establish churches, could both attest to her significant influence in their lives and ministries.

Not only did Priscilla serve the Lord and the church tirelessly, with her whole heart, but she did so living with great pressure. This was a time of intense persecution, and she literally risked her life for the Gospel, perhaps daily. A heart in bondage tries to save itself. Priscilla gave herself away. While we generally see men protect women, we see Priscilla protecting Paul, literally laying her life on the line for him.

Today Christ's followers everywhere find themselves living in an increasingly perilous world, as nightmarish terrorist attacks attest. In our culture, we are surrounded by people who have some knowledge of Jesus but who do not really know or understand His Gospel. Distortions of the Gospel are pervasive. While some are hostile to the truth, others simply wait to hear it. People need us to portray the Gospel to them in forthright and accurate ways. Like Priscilla, let's do what we can, not using excuses for hanging back and waiting for others to get the job done. Let's cast down our own self-serving preoccupations. With liberated hearts, let's lay ourselves wholly at Christ's feet. In a risky world, let's risk it all for His sake. He is worthy!

Liberated to Be Team Players

Teamwork is what makes marriages, churches, armies, and nations succeed. Thomas Jefferson spoke of teamwork when he said, "We mutually pledge to each other our lives, our fortunes, and our sacred honor." America is here today because of that type of commitment. When we studied Deborah and Esther, we saw two women on the frontlines. A significant factor in their lives was the incredible teamwork between them and the men God put in their lives. Deborah and Barak needed each other; Esther and Mordecai needed each other.

Here is another dynamic duo—this time a married couple. Priscilla and Aquila are sterling pillars of how a Christian marriage partnership should work. Their effectiveness together speaks to their relationship as a couple. Priscilla worked with Aquila as the Proverbs 31 woman whose "husband has full confidence in her and lacks nothing of value," who "brings him good, not harm, all the days of her life" (Prov. 31:11-12). Obviously, had she tried to outshine her husband or dominate him, God could not have used her effectively. She would never have earned the love and respect of all the churches.

Never competing but completing, Priscilla and Aquila functioned harmoniously as an extraordinarily effective husband-wife ministry team. Together in faith, interests, friendships, ministry, and sacrifice, they were true partners, showing how married couples can minister together.

They were not, however, just a team unto themselves. They partnered with Paul and the rest of the church for the sake of the Gospel. Paul was ever conspicuous, but they played their role inconspicuously. They stood with Paul, but they took a backseat. While he did the great public work, they did the great private work—praying, supporting, encouraging, nurturing. Everywhere they went—whether Corinth, Ephesus, or Rome—they used their home for God. Their hospitality opened the door of salvation to many as they invited people to gather there to study the Scriptures. As the church assembled in their home, and they discipled new believers, the church grew and became established. Paul was ever grateful to them and let everyone know it.

Those with independent, self-righteous, or competitive spirits can never be team players; neither can those who harbor anger, bitterness, or unforgiveness. They need the Lord to liberate their hearts. If we hope to be effective for God, we must do our part to make our relationships right. We need Christian friends and family. Especially in difficult times, the Christian community needs to stand together. This is an important function of the church. We share struggles with each other; we love and support each other. This is the beauty of being part of the body of Christ. How sad are the ones who, so concerned for and protective of "their" ministry, are not free to be team players.

Free Indeed

There is such freedom in a liberated heart! We can commit our disappointments, afflictions, and questions to the Lord. We trust God's promises. We accept others in love, forgive them, and walk with them. We accept honor or shame, success or failure. We are free from what others think of us; we overlook their responses and reactions. We are humble and teachable. We turn the other cheek, bless those who persecute us, give thanks in everything, and even accept the plundering of our possessions (Heb. 10:34). We are enabled to accept the seasons of our lives with grace. We let ourselves be broken and reshaped. We allow Christ to be formed in us. We follow God's call, no matter where it leads. We lay up our treasures in heaven. We rejoice in our trials. We command the enemy to flee, shatter his strongholds, and decimate his kingdom. We lay claim to the gifts and power of the Holy Spirit. We expect miracles, claiming great things from God and doing mighty things for Him. We soar on eagle's wings. We keep free of distractions, living for God with abandon. We keep our eyes on our goal. We are able to watch this world passing away before our eyes and not fear. We do not shrink from God's will; we do not bury our "talent" in the ground. We know that when we come to the other end of our Christian pilgrimage, we will be ready to see Christ face to face. Having been refined with fire, we will come forth like gold. Yes, with a liberated heart, we will have lived a liberated life. Then—praise God!—we will reign with Christ forever!

Priscilla was a blazing torch for Jesus in the Early Church. It was a time of miracles and missionary fervor and also a time of brutal persecution. Even thrown to lions, Christians like Priscilla had liberated hearts that put their enemies to shame. Their enemies tried to rub the church out of existence, but Priscilla, along with all her counterparts, kept God's kingdom advancing. Their enemies passed into history's wastebasket, but the first Christians changed the world for God's glory. Ultimately, the Roman Empire, along with all its gods, would succumb to the liberating power of the Gospel. We can thank Priscilla for the significant part she played in this triumph.

We, too, live in an opportune time for advancing God's kingdom. These are spiritually dark times, so ripe for a mighty move of God's Spirit. He will move in and through those who have allowed Him to prepare their hearts, those with liberated hearts. Many of God's people today live defeated and unfruitful lives. All over the world are people who need God and believers who need counsel, encouragement, exhortation, and prayer. God needs an army of Priscillas today to rise and move out in faith. With liberated hearts, we will see amazing things. Like Priscilla, we will change history.

Let's cry for God to deliver us from the false and passive postures that rob us of our authority in Christ. Let's cast off our fears in Jesus' name. Let's rise in winsome boldness to claim our rightful inheritance as God's children. Let's see ourselves seated in heavenly realms with Christ Jesus. Let's put on the armor of God and walk in resurrection power. With liberated hearts, let's shout, "If God be for us, who can be against us?" (Rom. 8:31). Let's declare, "Though an host should encamp against me, my heart shall not fear: though war should rise against me, in this will I be confident" (Ps. 27:3). Let's proclaim, "But thanks be to God, who in Christ always leads us in triumphal procession, and through us spreads the fragrance of the knowledge of him everywhere" (2 Cor. 2:14 ESV). Amen!

Heart Check

1. In what ways can you relate to Priscilla and to the conditions under which she lived?

2. What cultural restraints can keep us from effectively impacting our world for Christ?

3. Is there something the Lord has put in your heart to do for Him but you have not felt free to do it? What barriers do you see? Could the trouble arise from a need for a more liberated heart?

4. Can you think of any who inspire you by their liberated heart? How can you develop such a heart?

5. What about Priscilla's life most inspires you? How can you apply this to your own life?

6. Compose a prayer to God in response to this chapter's lessons.

7

The Woman with Two Mites

THE SACRIFICIAL HEART

MARK 12:41-44; LUKE 21:1-4

THE LORD HAS PROVIDED! The impoverished little widow smiled at the tiny coins in her hand. It was all the money she had in the world—not much but enough. How her heart rejoiced. What would she do with this money? Should she spend it immediately or put it in a jar and save it until she could add more? Most women in her position, who had to struggle so hard to make ends meet, needed to treasure every coin that came their way. But she had different ideas and didn't have to ponder a second. Her love for God compelled her. Putting on her threadbare cloak, she went out the door and made her way down the crowded, narrow Jerusalem streets toward the temple. *The Lord is so good to me*, she thought.

Arriving at the temple grounds, she headed toward the treasury. Lines of people waited their turn to put their offerings in the containers provided. Clutching her coins—she would not want to lose her precious treasure—she got in line. She watched as rich and poor alike gave their offerings. When it was her turn, she stepped up to the container and, with praise in her heart, released her coins. Then she walked away praying, *Thank You, Lord. I'm in Your hands completely.*

We call this woman's heart The Sacrificial Heart. By itself her offering was a mere pittance. Yet it represented a heart that loved God, one that gave all to Him. She left nothing for herself—a great and beautiful sacrifice. To a truly sacrificial heart, however, it is no sacrifice to give. She would not even have considered withholding from the God who sustained her and provided for her needs.

Perhaps she thought about the first time she had given sacrificially as a widow. It would have been much harder then. She may have wondered how she would get by. Perhaps she had to force herself to let go of her coins, hoping God would provide some way for her to survive. But provide He did. She had found Him to be ever faithful, and He had never let her down. He was her friend, her provider, her peace, her security . . . her everything.

Just two days before Passover, Jerusalem was a hubbub. Day by day the city grew more crowded as Jews from all over the known world flocked to the Holy City to celebrate the feast. Who would notice the little widow wending her way through the crowded streets and bazaars that day? She was insignificant, a face lost in the crowd. But someone did notice her, and because He did, her generous act would go down in history.

The outer court of the temple area (called the Court of the Gentiles) had the atmosphere of a county fair. There were pens for the sheep, goats, and oxen to be used in offerings. Above their bleating, baaing, and lowing, one could hear the sellers, loudly marketing their animals. Sellers of doves had their own area, as did the potters who provided customers with a huge assortment of clay dishes and ovens for roasting and eating their Passover lamb. There were also booths for everything else needed for the feast. The outer courts were even more crowded by the numerous people who used the temple grounds as a shortcut to wherever they were going. And then there were the infamous moneychangers busily changing foreign money into temple currency.

Pushing her way through the outer court, the widow moved through the Gate Beautiful, which gave access to the Court of

Women. Beyond this court, Jewish men could go on into the inner court, the Court of Israel. The Court of Women, however, was accessible to all Jews, and it contained the treasury where offerings were received. The treasury consisted of thirteen trumpet-shaped collection containers along the wall, each bearing an inscription that indicated to what use the donations would be put. Seven were designated for particular kinds of offerings—wood for burning the sacrifices, incense for burning on the altar, etc., and six were for freewill offerings.

Jesus was at the temple on this day. He had just finished teaching a large crowd in the Court of Women, probably near the treasury area as He sometimes did (see John 8:20). Though this was a time of feasting and celebration, Jesus was not feeling very festive. He had just warned His disciples: "Watch out for the teachers of the law. They like to walk around in flowing robes and be greeted in the marketplaces, and have the most important seats in the synagogues and the places of honor at banquets" (Mark 12:38-39). Jesus had pronounced woes on the religious leaders before (see Matt. 23:15, 16, 23, 25, 27, 29). Now giving fresh reason for condemning them, He added, "They devour *widows' houses* and for a show make lengthy prayers. Such men will be punished most severely" (Mark 12:40, emphasis mine).

Jesus considered charitableness to the poor a major duty of those who obey God. Not only did He preach good news to the poor (Luke 17:22), but He also commanded people to give to the poor (Mark 10:21; Luke 11:41), to invite the poor to their feasts (Luke 14:13), and even to sell their possessions in order to help the poor (Luke 12:33). And no one was more poor than Jerusalem's many widows. Jewish men who fell ill often wanted to be buried in Jerusalem; so many of them came from other regions, bringing with them their wives. When their husbands died, these widows were often left very poor and vulnerable to exploitation.

God abhors injustice. It infuriates Him when those in positions of trust use their power for their own gain, and particularly when it is at the expense of widows and orphans (Ex. 22:22-24). That's just what these religious leaders were doing. They persuaded widows that the best thing they could do was to give them their money, that doing so was an act of utmost piety. With no one to advise them, these widows were particularly susceptible to being stripped bare of everything they owned. Soon with all their resources gone, they were left distressed and broken.

Jesus saw this as extortion, literally as devouring widows' houses. The sin was even more reprehensible because the leaders cloaked their greed under the cover of religion. Their shows of piety and flowery prayers did not impress Jesus at all, and He predicted that these wicked men would be punished most severely.

After teaching the crowd, Jesus sat down in the temple treasury. He was particularly tired that day because in addition to His teaching, He had also been engaged in strenuous debates with emissaries of the Sanhedrin and also the Sadducees. Nevertheless, He wanted to make a further point to His disciples. He had exposed the hypocrisy and greed of the religious leaders, and now for contrast He would point out a good example.

The act of giving was always important to Jesus. "*Give* to the one who asks you" (Matt. 5:42, emphasis mine), He taught. "Freely you have received, freely *give*" (Matt. 10:8, emphasis mine). "*Give*, and it will be given to you" (Luke 6:38, emphasis mine). He, of course, modeled giving Himself: "Come to me . . . and I will *give* you rest" (Matt. 11:28, emphasis mine). "For even the Son of Man did not come to be served, but to . . . *give* his life as a ransom for many" (Mark 10:45, emphasis mine). "Whoever drinks the water I *give* him will never thirst" (John 4:14, emphasis mine). "I *give* them eternal life, and they shall never perish" (John 10:28, emphasis mine). Yes, He cared much about giving. His own sacrificial heart was about to lead him to give the ultimate sacrifice—His own life. In a few days He would begin His final journey through Jerusalem—up to Golgotha where He would give His life for the sins of the world.

Jesus sat opposite the donation receptacles where He could watch the stream of people dropping their money in. He often watched people, and as He did, He longed for them, wept for them, and sometimes rejoiced over them. Always He prayed for them. As He sat watching this day, He observed the rich and the poor and all in between.

Often the rich, decked in jewels and fine clothing, were particularly interested in being seen as they gave, emptying money boxes or even large bags of coins that clinked noticeably as they dropped into the receptacles. Jesus showed little emotion as He watched them leave. Those who made a scene, He knew, had received their full reward (see Matt. 6:2). Others, however, were not performing. They sincerely gave to God, and this pleased Jesus.

As Jesus and His disciples watched this parade of givers, suddenly His countenance brightened. He had found the perfect subject. Nothing could be worse to Him than those who devour a widow's substance. Yet nothing could be more praiseworthy to Him than what He was about to see. Waiting her turn was the poor little widow. She attracted no attention, but Jesus noticed her, and He saw what she had in her heart to do. To Him, she was a standout in the crowd, the most precious person He would see that day.

Though a poor widow, to be sure, in Jesus' eyes she was not a victim. On the contrary, this woman—so full of faith and love, so endued with a sacrificial heart—was a victor! Most women busily finished their last-minute shopping for their Passover meals, but here was one who didn't even have enough for a Passover meal. She did have enough for an offering though!

The Greco-Roman world had many coins, some made of costly silver and gold. But the widow's coins, called "lepta" (plural for lepton), were the lowest denomination of all in circulation. Smaller than the size of a dime, they probably weren't more than one-twelfth of a cent each. No wonder we call them "mites."

To Jesus, however, the monetary value of a donation was not of utmost importance. His standard for judging things is often contrary to everyone else's. Jesus evaluated gifts by the content of the heart. To Him, no one's heart that day measured up to the stature of this widow's heart. Her heart loved and trusted God so much that she would give everything she had to Him—gladly!

Some people counted out their coins as they drew near to the offering receptacles. But not her. When it was her turn, she approached the receptacle, opened her hand, looked at her two very small coins, and gave thanks. Then she dropped them into the receptacle. She had just given everything she had to God.

She never dreamed she was being watched in this selfless act of worship. She probably felt that she was the most insignificant person there, with the most insignificant gift. She did not realize that God-in-flesh sat a short distance away, watching her closely, with eyes sparkling and heart rejoicing. In the eyes of the world, the gifts of the rich were great and praiseworthy, while hers was puny and insignificant. In the eyes of Jesus, however, their gifts were relatively puny while her gift was immense, lavish, precious. He would not condemn anyone else's gift, but He would set hers far above every other one given that day. Despite the many defects in her coins due to hasty mintage methods, there was nothing cheap and worthless about her gift. Her sacrificial heart had just made two nearly worthless coins priceless!

What a lovely contrast this woman provided to the picture Jesus had just drawn of the hypocritical religious leaders. Loathing a piety that parades itself before the public eye for selfish gain, He had castigated their avarice, pomp, and show. By contrast, she had little to display and never expected to gain notice. In no way did selfishness prompt her. Out of sincere devotion, she simply came to worship God with what she had to give, knowing God as her Jehovah-jireh—her provider.

Pointing to this dear woman, Jesus said, "I tell you the truth, this poor widow has put more into the treasury than all the others" (Mark

12:43). He called her "poor." The word used here, *ptochos*, can be translated "poor" or "beggar." She was obviously poverty-stricken to the point of begging. Yet she was not begging—she was *giving*! And here was Jesus, declaring that she had given more than all the others. If we take Him literally, He was saying that she had put in more than all the others combined!

This statement amazed the disciples. How could a few mites compare with gold and silver? The love of money would always spell trouble for the church, and Jesus felt it of utmost importance to get His point across to His disciples now. One of them there had already sold out. Judas, a lover of money who stole from the common purse, must have considered the commendation of this pitiful widow incomprehensible and even distressing. Within days he would betray the Lord for silver coins (John 12:6; Matt. 26:15).

Jesus knew that His statement had shocked His disciples. So He explained, "They all gave out of their wealth; but she, out of her poverty, put in everything—all she had to live on" (Mark 12:44). He did not deny that the rich made generous contributions. The widow just gave more. If the Lord measures our gift by what is left over after we give, her kind of gift outdistances all others by far. For they gave out of their abundance and had plenty left after they gave. She, on the other hand, gave out of her scarcity and had nothing left. Denying herself in a way others knew nothing about, she gave not only her money but her heart, her trust, her future. In other words, she gave it all. What true sacrifice!

How different she was from the religious leaders who defrauded such people as herself. Christ's commendation for her was as great as His condemnation of them. They were rich; she was poor. They were self-centered; she was God-centered. They gave superficially; she gave sacrificially. While they paraded what they supposedly gave to God, she simply gave in faith out of love for God. She did not try to impress anyone. She did not want to make a scene. How she had put them to shame!

Of course, the one with the greatest sacrificial heart of all, the one who within days would pay the ultimate sacrifice for all of us, was Jesus Himself. How He cherished this woman's sacrificial heart.

Listen, my beloved brothers and sisters. Has not God chosen the poor in the world to be rich in faith and to be heirs of the kingdom that he has promised to those who love him?

JAMES 2:5 NRSV

As Jesus left the temple with His disciples, the disciples showed just how little they understood their Master's point. Immediately they began to remark about what they thought mattered to God. Fixating again on the great, the grandiose, the lofty, one of them said of the temple, "Look, Teacher! What massive stones! What magnificent buildings!" (Mark 13:1). This must have frustrated the Lord so soon after pointing out the difference between what God esteems and what man esteems. The temple of a simple heart that loves God means inestimably more to Jesus than the most grandiose showpiece on earth. Jesus replied to His disciple that the entire temple compound would be torn down completely. Oh, but the temple of a human heart that reverences God—now that remains forever!

No one but Jesus would have noticed the little widow in the temple that day, and certainly no one but Jesus noticed the soft plink of her tiny coins. Yet to Him, they fell into the offering box with a resounding crash. He would make certain that sound would be heard throughout the world. Down through the ages those two little mites would be multiplied a hundred, a thousand, a million, a billionfold. Not only did her gift bless the heart of Jesus that day, but it has also blessed the hearts of countless others in every generation. Today the world knows more about this poor widow's gift than about the gift of the richest person in Israel at that time. To this very hour, her sacrificial heart still moves multitudes toward the Lord's treasury, inspiring them with faith to open their hearts and wallets and give sacrificially to God.

Had the widow heard the praise Jesus heaped on her that day? She may not have been at all aware of it. She had not looked for praise anyway. She went home with a song in her heart: *Thank You, Lord, that You always provide me with an offering. I love You.*

LESSONS FOR OUR OWN HEARTS

The law from your mouth is more precious to me than thousands of pieces of silver and gold.

PSALM 119:72

Imagine Bill Gates walking into the Jerusalem temple that day with his money box. Things couldn't get much more exciting! After all, he's worth a modest $59 million—oops, make that billion! Just how generous would he be? Well, in the year 2000 he gave more than $5 billion to his foundation, which then dispersed close to $1 billion to various charities. As impressive as this is, guess what? If he had walked up to the temple collection box and put this same sum inside, Jesus still would have found the widow's gift more striking.

Can you imagine it? Jesus prefers to hold up as a model of generosity a woman who gave less than a cent! A little widow who cheerfully and freely says, "Take it all, Lord," sways His heart more than the world's richest philanthropist, who has some $54 billion left sitting around for himself after his donation. By God's calculator, she is vastly more charitable. Think about that, the rest of you 537 billionaires in the world today! Amazingly, when it comes to the domain of human hearts, every person has an equal opportunity to please God.

. . . poor, yet making many rich; having nothing, and yet possessing everything.

2 CORINTHIANS 6:10

I know your afflictions and your poverty—yet you are rich!

REVELATION 2:9

This generous widow's story never fails to touch hearts. It is easy, however, to think, *How sweet of Jesus to recognize this simple woman.* But there is nothing sweet and tender about this account. It is a story of raw courage and triumph, the story of a woman with grit, fortitude, and unassailable determination to honor God.

It is also easy to think of the widow's mite as a very small amount. Listen to the words of a few hymns: "If you cannot give your thousands,/You can give the widow's mite./What you truly give for Jesus,/Will be precious in His sight" and "Yet when Thou dost accept their gold, Lord, treasure up my mite." Did the writers really mean to equate their gifts with the widow's gift? Are they really giving everything? Let's be careful not to miss the real message—that this woman gave a *great* amount when she gave everything to God. This hymn captures the truest sense of the story: "Take my silver and my gold;/not a mite would I withhold."[1]

Not only does God's Word tell us about the widow and her gift, but it also shows us Christ's profound interest in giving habits. On that day He was concerned with His preaching and teaching and with refuting those who argued with Him. He was also, no doubt, concerned with His imminent death on the cross. Yet He sat there studying the givers at the temple. He knew what each gave and with what heart they gave it. He knows how we give, too.

When we go to church, we might think that the Lord is impressed with our friendliness or the intensity with which we sing or pray or take sermon notes. Even if we try to distract Him with our other expressions of piety, however, He still watches closely as the offering plate goes by. Not only does He watch what we put in, but He watches what we do not put in. He knows percentages and proportions. He knows the entries in our checkbooks. That's what tests the reality of what we profess. That's what proves our priorities. Have we given generously or stingily, gladly or grudgingly, in proportion to what He deserves or to what we think we will have left after we satisfy our own wants? He knows.

The widow was a New Testament giver while still under the Old Testament Law. The Law required a 10 percent tithe (Lev. 27:30, 32). Thus the tithe is not really a New Testament concept. The New Testament concept is that everything we have is God's, and from that reality we give back to Him. The Law does not regulate our giving; love does. The law of love starts at 10 percent and goes up from there. The beauty of giving in God's economy is that the poor can give the same percentage as the rich, and that is how God sees it. For the widow, 10 percent was too small a sacrifice. So was 20 or 30 percent. She had to give it all. She wanted God to have 100 percent because she considered Him worthy. That's a sacrificial heart!

Money in itself holds no value with God. When you think about it, assuming we could give anything to the God of the universe almost seems absurd. Isn't it obvious that it is all His anyway? "The God who made the world and everything in it . . . is not served by human hands, as if he needed anything, because he himself gives all men life and breath and everything else" (Acts 17:24-25). Everything we possess—and think of the magnitude of His gift to us!—has been filtered through His grace. How then can we hold anything back when we owe Him *everything?* Think a moment about the words of another old hymn:

> *When I survey the wondrous cross*
> *On which the Prince of glory died,*
> *My richest gain I count but loss,*
> *And pour contempt on all my pride.*
>
> *Forbid it, Lord, that I should boast,*
> *Save in the death of Christ my God!*
> *All the vain things that charm me most,*
> *I sacrifice them to His blood.*

Were the whole realm of nature mine,
That were a present far too small:
Love so amazing, so divine,
Demands my soul, my life, my all.

ISAAC WATTS

The little widow is a wonderful and inspiring example to us all. I am really happy to say that I know people who have followed her example to an amazing degree, and what inspiration and joy I derive from their stories. I have missionary friends from my own church who have given up a lifestyle of affluence and comfort to serve in difficult places such as Pakistan and Africa, living on very little, and who still send back their tithes and offerings to the church!

According to an annual giving survey, there may be a looming financial crisis for churches due to changing attitudes toward the offering plate. Giving dropped significantly in 2000. Even among born-again Christians, contributions declined 16 percent from the previous year, and a mere 12 percent tithed. Since the "baby buster" generation (twenties to mid-thirties) give very little, things could keep getting worse.[2] As Christians, we should give generously. If we are rich Christians, we should give lavishly. What we give materially to God reflects how much love we have in our hearts for Him.

The widow gave until she could give no more. How many Christians miserly calculate what they can afford to give God. Their question is not truly, "What can I give?" but "What can I get away with not giving?" This is not giving from the heart. How is it that the world has philanthropists who love to give charitably, and yet many of God's own people are tight-fisted? We may fight fiercely for orthodoxy, but when it comes to this area, many of us are functionally agnostics. Just what kind of Christians are we when we begrudge every dollar spent for Christ and His church, when we toss a token amount in the offering plate, when we adopt the motto: "Charity begins at home and ends there, too."

Paul, speaking of such mysteries, says, "For it is not those who hear the law who are righteous in God's sight, but it is those who obey the law who will be declared righteous. Indeed, when Gentiles, who do not have the law, do by nature things required by the law, they are a law for themselves . . . since they show that the requirements of the law are written on their hearts . . ." (Rom. 2:13-15). Why is it that so many of God's own people don't have God's law written in their hearts?

Every day we make choices. Look at the widow again. Some say that according to the rules of that day, one could not put less than two mites in the temple offering. If that is true, then she had a choice between keeping it all for herself or giving it all to God. She could not choose to halve it. What would we have done? Honestly, wouldn't most of us have justified keeping it all? "Lord, I know you understand. When I can, I'll give a good offering to you." But the widow chose God. Showing Him gratitude was more important than buying food. No wonder she tugged the Lord's heartstrings!

Some of us seem to think we have a special dispensation from God not to give sacrificially to Him. We hear the sermons and hope to tithe someday. We complain that we *can't* tithe because we simply can't afford to. Some point to their many outstanding bills—payments for their large homes, luxury cars, boat, vacations. Others truly don't have much to give and cry, "If we could just get out of debt, then we'd tithe." But God tests our hearts to see if we will put our money where our mouth is. Suddenly the house gets refinanced, a new job presents itself, or an inheritance comes through. Now they can change their giving habits, right? Do they? Usually not.

Try explaining proper stewardship to these folk, and you'll hear back, "Well, you just don't understand." In other words, "You don't understand; my pastor doesn't understand; no one understands—but God does." They will even say straight out, "God understands!" But while the Lord does have a great measure of grace for us, I doubt that He really "understands" when we toss Him our scraps. What He *does* understand is that we are untrusting and greedy, and it grieves Him.

If we cannot trust God with our finances, how can we truly say we trust Him at all? How can we call Him the Lord of our lives if He's not Lord of our money? Do we honor Him when we doubt that He is great enough to provide for us or that He loves us enough or that He stands by the promises of His word? Our actions tell Him what we *do* believe—that He is unimportant, incapable, unloving, and unwise. So we should fend for ourselves. In essence, we say, "Thank You, Lord, for offering to be my Lord, but I really think I can do a better job of managing my money than You can. I'm sure You understand."

> *Will anyone rob God? Yet you are robbing me! But you say, "How are we robbing you?" In your tithes and offerings! You are cursed with a curse, for you are robbing me—the whole nation of you! Bring the full tithe into the storehouse, so that there may be food in my house, and thus put me to the test, says the LORD of hosts; see if I will not open the windows of heaven for you and pour down for you an overflowing blessing.*
>
> MALACHI 3:8-10 NRSV

God does not always make it easy for His children to obey Him. He asks us to do difficult things, to weather the storms and pains of life, and still to trust Him and even to sacrifice our lives for Him. Giving financially is just a token of giving our entire lives to Christ. The widow knew what it was to struggle. Yet she gave. That's trust. That's maturity. That's a triumphant heart!

Those who dare to give to God, who with sacrificial hearts offer their very lives and fortunes to Him, have learned some important things.

To Give No Matter What

Besides giving to the Lord because He is worthy, we need to give so that we can be more like Him. He wants us to give for our benefit, so we can be free from ourselves and free to partner with Him in His mission in this world. He wants us to bear the fruit of love.

The Lord knows our hearts, and He knows our excuses for not giving. Perhaps we feel poor. Perhaps we really *are* poor—a widow, a divorcee, or we may be jobless or deeply in debt. But we should not use this as an excuse for not giving to God. There is a story of a missionary who taught the native converts all the right stuff, or so it seemed. One day the missionary had a conversation with the Lord:

"Lord, I think my task here is finished. I've taught them everything I know."

"You missed something."

"What?"

"You forgot to tell them about giving."

"Oh, Lord, these people are so poor they don't have anything to give. That's why I avoided teaching them about giving."

"I want you to teach them about giving."

So the missionary did as the Lord said. The natives received the word with joy. Out of their great poverty, they came to the little church with whatever they had—one with an egg, another with a bit of produce. The joy of the Lord was released in powerful ways as these natives learned to partner with God in giving.

The Lord is always watching and caring for us. He loves us, but He often has to push us out of our cozy nests so we can learn to fly. In times of darkness, when we feel uncertain and fearful, we need to let faith shine and trust God as our provider. I'm thankful that my husband stressed to our children in their formative years that God is their provider. Their faith in Him has allowed them to step out and do radical things for Him. If you think *you* are your provider, then you will only do what is reasonable in your mind, and you will miss out on God's supernatural provision.

The widow knew that the source of her provision was not her coins but her God. The Lord knows where we find our security, too. Until we make Him our security, we will never feel truly secure. Perhaps we need to have idolatry broken in our lives. If we trust in earthly securities more than in God, that is idolatry. That was the rich

young ruler's problem. Christ loved him, but he still went away
empty because of the things he could not bring himself to relinquish.
He wanted to follow Jesus—then again, he did not. If an impoverished little widow could give it all, why couldn't he? Because she
trusted God while he trusted his idols.

This is a hard word, isn't it? It's hard to surrender everything. It's
hard to trust the Lord *that* much. Until we do though, we are in
bondage. We need to see that God does not intend to squelch us but
to free us. Life is unpredictable. We can't count on what might happen the next moment. When we are freed in Christ, we know that
true security can only be found in God and that every other security
will ultimately fail us. We might come to the end of our resources
suddenly, but God is trustworthy. The little widow knew the freedom
of a child of God who leans wholly upon the Lord.

No matter what we have or don't have, God always provides us
with something to give. Give then. Give your time, your effort, your
gifts, your talents, and your money. Learn to depend upon God to
make up the difference. It is as we get in over our heads, rather than
playing it safe, that we learn dependence. When we give sacrificially,
we learn to depend on God, rather than on ourselves.

To Give from the Heart

The act of sacrificial giving comes from a sacrificial heart. Without a
sacrificial heart, one cannot truly give with abandon. The widow
emptied herself out for God, all she had and all she was. God delights
in that kind of sacrificial heart. When we give with a sacrificial heart,
who knows what miracle might spring from it?

Dr. David Yonghi Cho, pastor of the world's largest church, likes
to tell the story of an elderly woman in his church who kicked off the
fundraising drive for their mammoth church building. After challenging the people to give what they had, he suddenly saw a poor old
woman come running down to the front of the church to offer what
she had—an empty rice bowl. Her sacrificial gift ignited a spirit of giv-

ing in the church, enabling them to build. When Clay visited this church years ago, he watched in amazement as 25,000 people flocked into that facility (with another 25,000 in overflow rooms) on a Sunday morning for one of the seven or eight services, all filled to capacity.

Sacrificial hearts will always find a way to give. Greedy hearts will always find a way to gain. Did the widow who gave her mites leave the temple to become rich? Did she get one hundredfold on her "investment"? I don't know. What we do know is that the Lord said in Deuteronomy 15:11 that there would always be poor people in the land and that we should help them out. The Early Church didn't go to widows like this one and say, "Give all you have to us, and God will bless you one hundredfold." Instead, they provided for their widows.

We should watch our motives for giving. If we keep the widow with her two mites in mind, we will be careful about what we call a sacrificial gift. She had no strings attached. She just wanted to give because God is worthy. A true gift of love comes from a sacrificial heart that willingly sacrifices to see God honored. Sacrificial giving is giving until it begins to hurt. It means choosing to do without. Look at these definitions of sacrifice from the *American Heritage Dictionary*: "Forfeiture of something highly valued for the sake of one considered to have a greater value or claim; to sell or give away at a loss." This is devotion. Many a groom will present his bride with a ring that he obtained at great sacrifice. How much more should we love God!

To Give Until It Feels Good

What if everyone had given sacrificially like the widow that day at the Jerusalem temple? What if all God's people gave to the Lord's work with sacrificial hearts today? I can almost hear someone say, "Then we'd all be in the poorhouse!" Such are the thoughts of those who have not yet learned to live a sacrificial life. One with a sacrificial heart does not walk around in agony. No! More than likely, this person experiences God's pleasure, His blessing, and may even see mighty miracles as a result of the sacrifice. There is joy as a result of giving to

God, not remorse. Even if we go through some agony in the interim period, we still know joy is coming. Jesus paid the ultimate sacrifice with His life, but He did it for the joy set before Him (Heb. 12:2).

Stories in the book of Acts provide us with stirring glimpses of the sacrificial nature of the Early Church: "Selling their possessions and goods, they gave to anyone as he had need. . . . Much grace was upon them all. There were no needy persons among them. For from time to time those who owned lands or houses sold them, brought the money from the sales and put it at the apostles' feet, and it was distributed to anyone as he had need" (Acts 2:45; 4:33-35).

Even more stirring, however, is the heart of the impoverished Macedonian church: "And now, brothers, we want you to know about the grace that God has given the Macedonian churches. Out of the *most severe trial*, their *overflowing joy* and their *extreme poverty* welled up in *rich generosity*. For I testify that *they gave as much as they were able*, and *even beyond their ability*. Entirely on their own, *they urgently pleaded* with us *for the privilege of sharing* in this service to the saints" (2 Cor. 8:1-4, emphasis mine). There you have it. As much as the phrases in this report seem to conflict with each other, they do not. These sisters and brothers embraced the call to give, and with sacrificial hearts, not only gave beyond all reason, but did it with great joy, counting it a privilege. It felt great!

I have often gotten excited about the "much grace" (or "great grace," KJV) spoken of in Acts 4:33. "Lord, send that great grace that turns the world upside down for You; send the power of Your Spirit—the signs, wonders, salvation, joy, intensity fire, rain—send it!" I failed to see, however, just how much sacrificial giving was a key expression of that grace. Perhaps I never saw it because I didn't want to see it! Look again at the Macedonian church: "the *grace* that God has given the Macedonian churches." Their overwhelming generosity was an outflow of God's grace. Let's pray for more of *this* kind of grace! As we know, grace must be received to become activated.

Continuing with his message to the Corinthians about giving,

Paul says, "The point is this: the one who sows sparingly will also reap sparingly, and the one who sows bountifully will also reap bountifully. Each of you must give as you have made up your mind, not reluctantly or under compulsion, for God loves a cheerful giver. And God is able to provide you with every blessing in abundance, so that by always having enough of everything, you may share abundantly in every good work. . . . Thanks be to God for his indescribable gift!" (2 Cor. 9:6-8, 15 NRSV).

Paul described the principle of sowing and reaping. We sow our resources into God's kingdom, and He gives back so that we have enough for our need, but also enough to sow back more into His kingdom. Blessings just keep flowing as we freely enter this cycle of giving. Our life becomes a joyous adventure. If, on the other hand, tithes and offerings must be pulled out of us, then we miss the joy.

Let me tell you a bit of my story. I must admit that Clay is the real giver in our home, and I have largely come along for the ride. I've come a long way though. Clay's story starts back when, as a seminary student, he heard a sermon about tithing that struck him to his core. Prior to this, he reasoned, "I'm just a poor seminary student who is giving his whole life to God. Surely He doesn't expect more than that from me." The sermon convinced him, however, to commit for the rest of his life to always give at least 10 percent back to God. It's been some thirty years since then, and Clay has never backed off from that commitment. He set an example to our children and to me. We had few luxuries, and many of our clothes were secondhand. Nevertheless, we always looked nice and had enough for the essentials. We always gave at least 10 percent off the top of our income.

Sometimes when we struggled financially, I was less than happy about tithing. God always provided for us though. But then Clay wanted to up our giving to 15 percent. I went along but was not a cheerful giver. We had never owned a house, and every door always seemed to slam in our face when we wanted to buy one. I had worked part time, but my heart was in ministry. Clay and I had determined that we would never become enslaved to a home, that if I had to take full-time employment for us to buy a home, we just wouldn't own one. As soon as we decided in secret to increase our giving, however, friends came out of the woodwork to help us into a home. One gave us stocks worth about $9,000. We made an offer on a house, trusting in faith that God would provide the $4,500 we didn't have to complete the deal. Within seven days of making the offer, the stock value rose from $9,000 to $13,500. Exactly $4,500!

Sometime later the Lord called us to northern California. We rented for eight years. We liked where we were and never had the money to get a house we could both agree on. Clay continued to increase our giving, and, as usual, I went along with him. Then our church got the increasing sense that we should embark on a huge building program. We were bursting at the seams and desperately needed more space. Clay did not want to get into a building program, but the Lord kept pressing the point, and the church voted to build a building and try to stay out of debt, at least until the project's final phase. That meant we had to have a huge pledge drive, pledging amounts we would give over a three-year period.

Clay and I, along with most others in the church, prayed about what to pledge. We lived frugally, nearly from paycheck to paycheck, and already gave 15 percent. So I worked it out in my head that we could possibly afford to pledge $3,000. I thought this was quite generous actually. Clay came home after praying about it though and said, "Honey, I think we're supposed to pledge $20,000."

How did I react? Well, how do you think I reacted? I could not believe my ears! We still didn't have a house, drove clunkers, bought bargain foods at the food outlet, and purchased many of our clothes at thrift stores. I had finally had enough. When it came to finances, I did not have a sacrificial heart, nor had I ever. It was just too much.

I flew into a tantrum. Clay tried to explain: "We've got to set an example to the church. If we aren't generous, then no one else will be." I didn't care. I just kept fuming. Finally he said, "Honey, this is a *faith* pledge. If the money isn't there, we just can't give it. If God provides, we'll give it."

Our building project was called "Faith Adventure," and suddenly I began to catch hold of the adventure. It was up to *God*, not me. I just needed to cooperate with Him as He provided. "Okay," I said, "it's up to God. We'll see what He does."

Immediately we raised our giving to what amounted to between 20-25 percent. We were giving beyond our means. This took us into the realm of faith. Three years later we testified to the church that not only had we given the $20,000, but we had even gained financially! The first week we made that pledge, we received a wonderful car from a relative. Later someone else gave me an expensive computer. One year into the pledge, we found that we could change our medical insurance and save $5,000 per year. Also we started getting voluntarily bumped on our airline flights. By the end of three years, we had flown *thousands* of dollars worth of free flights, some of those even with first-class tickets!

Nevertheless, I breathed a sigh of relief at the end of the three-year pledge drive. Now I thought we could relax. Then it became evident that the church needed more money for the building. The situation called for another two-year pledge drive. This time I didn't have a fit when Clay came home and said we needed to pledge another $10,000. I just sighed and said, "We'll never own a house again."

Within two weeks of this pledge, a man in our church who was leaving the area called Clay and asked if we would like to pray about buying his house. It hadn't sold, and he was desperate. He would gladly sell it to us for what he had paid for it. Clay informed him that he would at least pray about it, but that it was out of our price range. Clay figured that we would need another $20,000 as down payment to enable us to buy that home without decreasing our giving. He hung up the phone, and *two seconds* later it rang again. This time it was a woman not related to our church, who wasn't even a Christian at the time. "Clay, do you need help buying a house?" she asked. "I want to give you and Cheri $20,000 to help you buy a house."

God gave us a beautiful house! After the pledge drives were over, Clay said, "Cheri, I never want to go backward in our giving. Life is too exciting this way!" Well, I can report to you that we still give generously to God, and the adventure just keeps getting better all the time. That's because my husband is a cheerful giver, and I'm becoming one. We never gave in order to get blessings in return, but they've come pouring in. God proved and continues to prove the truth of His Word to us. There is no doubt at all in our minds that I would not be sitting at this computer in this lovely home today if we had not learned to give sacrificially.

Now I understand, more than ever before, the sad state we are in when we clutch our resources and, in so doing, clog the channel of God's blessing. I am so thankful for a husband with a sacrificial heart who delights in giving to God. Our lives have been like an old coal train. It took awhile for that train to get up its steam. For many years, we were crawling down the tracks. But we kept burning the fuel, and God kept shoveling in more. Our train picked up steam and kept traveling faster. Now we're burning up the tracks! What an adventure!

Honor the LORD *with your wealth, with the firstfruits of all your crops; then your barns will be filled to overflowing, and your vats will brim over with new wine.*

PROVERBS 3:9-10

One man gives freely, yet gains even more; another withholds unduly, but comes to poverty.

PROVERBS 11:24

Let's look again at that statement, "God loves a *cheerful* giver." The Greek word used here, *hilaros,* from which we get our word "hilarious," indicates great merriment. What joy those with sacrificial hearts derive from their giving! Dare I say that I am becoming one of those "hilarious" givers?

Be an Example to Others

Generally, giving is best done in secret. But sometimes—when our hearts are right—we should make it public. Clay stood before our congregation at the beginning of our "Faith Adventure" and told how much we had pledged. His example of faith encouraged many others to step out in faith as well. At the end he was able to testify that we had given, by God's grace, the entire $20,000. He then told all the ways God had given back to us.

Some might wonder if these things should have been kept private between us and God. The answer is no. Why shouldn't God be honored for His faithfulness? Isn't it interesting that Paul urged Timothy to "set an example for the believers in speech, in life, in love, in faith and in purity" (1 Tim. 4:12). Does this include being an example in giving? Of course it does. Where did we get the idea that we should always keep our giving habits under a veil of secrecy?

True, Jesus implied that if we give so we can impress people and show our piety with a public display, we had better do it in secret. But many times in Scripture, public examples of generosity served as a tremendous inspiration to others—David and Israel's leaders (1 Chron. 29:2-9); Barnabas (Acts 4:36-37); Paul, Silas, and Timothy (2 Thess. 3:7-9); a centurion (Luke 7:4-5); Mary of Bethany (John 12:3)—just to mention a few. On the other hand, Ananias and Sapphira got into trouble for their public deception. They *pretended* to give more than they actually did. The issue here was not the amount but their heart motive. How many Christians today like to give the appearance of generosity but actually give very little, and they hide their stinginess by maintaining that giving should be in secret.

I think it would amaze us to open the ledgers and find out the real givers in the church. Some people of means, who we assume give much, actually give little; others who have little, who we assume give little, give sacrificially. Exposing this information would totally humiliate some of us. Yet don't we know that one day soon the ledgers really *will* be opened when we stand before God and all of heaven. If we fear exposure now, why not then?

Some in our church, to their loss, never caught the vision for our "Faith Adventure." Many others, however, jumped on board and gave liberally. Some of the more wealthy folk amazed us, giving very generously, and we couldn't have done it without them. But the widows really shined. One little lady, Laurie Woodruff, on a small fixed income, had a sacrificial heart. After making a sizeable pledge already, she testified before the congregation that she was canceling a magazine subscription for three years so she could give even more!

Recently she passed on to be with Jesus at the age of ninety-one. Her last words on earth were: "Rejoice! Rejoice!" Laurie knew the joy of living sacrificially for Jesus. It was people like her who spurred on our congregation of five hundred, many of whom were students, to raise more than $1.6 million.

As the people of God, we sit here on the edge of history today. Things are wrapping up in this old world, and we desperately need to see a mighty move of God's Spirit sweeping the earth. Someone has challenged: "Would you have an awakening in your community, your church, your own lives; then become the fuel, and a revival fire will be the result." Let's take that challenge. Let's become the fuel for God's fire. Let's pour our whole lives—everything we are, everything we have—into the Lord's work in these end times.

If we let God form in us truly sacrificial hearts, we may see the heavens open miraculously in the area of our provision. He tests our hearts and watches for those who are trustworthy stewards of His provision. "For the eyes of the LORD range throughout the earth to strengthen those whose hearts are fully committed to him" (2 Chron. 16:9). It is our heavenly Father's desire to give us all things: "He who did not spare his own Son, but gave him up for us all—how will he not also, along with him, graciously give us all things?" (Rom. 8:32). He wants to show Himself strong in our behalf. He wants to honor us and to give us a spirit of freedom, adventure, and joy. He wants to release plenteous resources to us, to bless us so we can be a blessing in the earth (see Gen. 12:1-3 and Deut. 8:18). But we must permit that flow of blessing by responding to His call with sacrificial hearts.

God loves to bless His children, and when He blesses us, He does not want us to feel guilty, but glad and grateful. But we must always keep our hands and hearts open to how He might want to use our resources for His kingdom. In a time when churches are awed by the great, the flamboyant, the showy, there are so many traps and snares. We must remember that large incomes, large congregations, large structures do not necessarily impress God. I learned early on in our building program that the building was secondary to the work God was doing in our hearts. It's the radicals like the woman with her two mites that most impress God.

Most people looked at this little woman and saw poverty; Christ saw liberty. Most people might have seen her act as reckless, but Christ saw faith and love in action. Most people call her gift "the widow's mite;" I think Christ calls it "the widow's might." Let's be mighty for God, too. Let's allow the Holy Spirit to get down to our hearts so He can shake us from our self-deception and ignite within us a new passion for Christ. Let's give with sacrificial hearts to His interests. As we measure our gifts, let's remember to measure them not by what we give, but by what we keep. I hope you won't miss the blessing. Let the little Jerusalem widow whom the Lord commended hold a spiritual mirror to your heart, helping you to assess its condition. She kept nothing for herself; she gave it all away. What a heart!

Do not store up for yourselves treasures on earth, where moth and rust destroy, and where thieves break in and steal. But store up for yourselves treasures in heaven, where moth and rust do not destroy, and where thieves do not break in and steal. For where your treasure is, there your heart will be also.

MATTHEW 6:19-21

Heart Check

1. Some might consider this a sweet story, and others might feel threatened by it. How does it make you feel?

2. How do you rank your monetary priorities? Does your giving pattern reflect your priorities?

3. Do you give regularly to God? Do you do so grudgingly or gratefully, stingily or sacrificially?

4. Can you think of an instance when you triumphed in the area of financial stewardship?

5. Read Psalm 37:16-26 and 1 Timothy 6:5-11. How does surrendering to the Lord in the area of our finances hold the promise of joyful living?

6. Compose a prayer in response to this chapter's lessons.

8

The Woman at the Well

THE GOOD-NEWS HEART

JOHN 4:4-42

THE EXCITED WOMAN flew along the road with the gait of an athlete. Except for her hem, which she held high enough for her sandaled feet to pound the ground freely, she was empty-handed. She was not empty-hearted though. A great exultation filled it nearly to bursting. She could barely believe what she had just experienced.

Only an hour before, she had passed this same way. Then she had trudged over the hot, dry ground, shoulders drooping, gait slow and unsteady. Tired to death, with a heart more dead than alive, she had felt like a burnt-out old woman, thinking only of her parched lips and aching feet. But now *everything* had changed! Now the dull gray terrain exploded with color. Her once-worn face glowed, her dreary eyes danced, and her downcast spirit sang for joy. It had been years since she had felt such excitement. In fact, nothing had *ever* excited her like the events of this hour—not even her first wedding! *Run faster!* she told herself. *I've got to get home! I've got to tell EVERYONE!*

She had been a sinful woman, unworthy of redeeming. No one in her town thought she had any future—least of all herself. Although she had longed for a new way of life, it seemed too late for her. But she had just met someone who claimed—and whom she believed—to be the Messiah. The new life she thought unreachable had come to her. In one short visit, this man named Jesus had somehow known all her failures and sin. Yet He gave her no tongue-lashing or moral lecture—just an incredible invitation. He offered to rescue her from hopeless futility and enable her to break free from her past into a gloriously transformed life full of hope. Such good news!

She knew, however, that she could not keep such good news to herself; she had to tell her neighbors about Jesus. Overcoming many obstacles to sharing her faith—embarrassment, shame, resentment, selfishness, and complacency, to name a few—she felt joyously compelled to tell *everyone,* friends and enemies alike. We call her heart The Good News Heart. Let's look more closely at her story.

It was late morning when she hoisted her clay pot onto her head with an unhappy sigh. Getting the daily supply of water was women's work—*poor* women's work. Women of means did not draw water. Her pot felt heavier than usual as she balanced it, though not as heavy as her heart. As she left the courtyard to do this daily chore, she felt only a hollow loneliness.

Jacob's well, situated at the northeastern foot of Mount Gerizim in Samaria, was a one-mile trek from her hometown of Sychar, which lay at the southern base of Mount Ebal. As she crossed the valley between these two mountains, the sweltering sun beat upon her, making her all the more unhappy.

Other women had either gone to the well earlier or would wait till it was cooler. But she came now to avoid cold stares. She felt like a total failure for whom no one in the world cared. So she came to the well at the time of least traffic—high noon.

This woman had married five times, strong evidence that she had experienced repeated heartbreaks, and the wounds went deep. Perhaps some of her husbands had died, but more likely they had divorced her. As a woman, she could not initiate a divorce; only men had that right (see Deut. 24:1-4). Hillel, a Palestinian rabbi of the period who greatly influenced the interpretation of Judaic law, interpreted Scriptures to mean that anything displeasing about a wife, regardless of its insignificance, was grounds for divorce. Perhaps this woman had been a terrible wife, maybe even unfaithful. On the other hand, perhaps she had been passed from husband to husband for as little as habitually burning the toast!

Heartache and age had taken its toll. After being rejected and shamed by five men, perhaps she had given up on marriage. But a single woman in this culture might starve without a man, so she got herself a man, this time simply cohabiting with him.

As she tramped toward the well, Mount Gerizim's 3,000-foot peak loomed large before her. It was both a symbol of hope and a point of mystery. As she looked up at it, she may have wondered, *Is God up there somewhere?*

Suddenly a noisy group of people coming down the road interrupted her thoughts. They were still far off and had not yet noticed her. Soon she could see that they were men, nearly a dozen of them. She trembled. *Can't run. Just keep walking. . . . Oh, no! They're Jews!* A Samaritan, she hated Jews, just like the rest of her people. Her heart beat wildly as they met on the road, but she could see their aversion for her. No need to worry; they wouldn't touch her for anything. As they passed each other without a word, she thought, *They think they're so righteous. Well, I loathe them!*

Jesus had walked in the hot sun that day, too. Passing through Samaria on His way from Judea to go minister in Galilee, He came to Jacob's well. Like all active wells in the East, it doubtless had a shelter from the sun with stone seats. Tired from His journey, He decided to rest there while His disciples went into town.

Although this was the quickest route from Judea to Galilee, most Jews elected to take the long route around Samaria. Despite its rich historical significance to the Jews—Jacob's well itself was an important site, thought to be the oldest well in the world—they went to great lengths to skirt the territory. Why? Simply to avoid contact with the Samaritans, whom they hated.

Jews and Samaritans were bitter enemies. Their hostility went back some seven hundred years to when there were two Jewish kingdoms, Israel in the north and Judah in the south. The Assyrians conquered the northern kingdom and immediately moved to prevent uprisings in the territory by deporting much of the Jewish population—primarily the rich and educated classes who could keep Jewish nationalism alive. After moving them to distant regions of the empire, the Assyrians then colonized the land with non-Jewish foreigners from other conquered territories. Intermarriages between these people and the Jews remaining in Israel resulted in the people known as Samaritans. In strict Jewish homes, a child who married a Gentile lost the right even to be called a Jew, having committed an unforgivable crime. Samaritans, therefore, were completely impure in the eyes of the Jews living in Judah. Not only that, their mingling of religious and cultural traditions resulted in a religion that was a mishmash of Jewish and pagan religion (see 2 Kings 17:22-34).

When southern Jews of Judah were overtaken and exiled to Babylon, about 140 years later, they remained steadfastly Jewish. Later Cyrus, king of Persia, permitted the exiled Jews to return and rebuild the Jerusalem temple. Samaritans offered to help them, but the Jews refused their offer. These pure Jews believed that the Samaritans represented a betrayal of their God and their heritage.

Open enmity between the two peoples sprang up, and the Samaritans broke fellowship with Jews and opposed the rebuilding. Setting up a rival religious system, they built their own temple on Mount Gerizim. They worshiped God according to their own traditions, accepting only the Pentateuch (first five books of the Bible) as God's Word.

Throughout the centuries, the rabid hostilities continued. When the Syrian Antiochus persecuted the Jews, the Samaritans stood aside. Later the Jews attacked Samaria, sacking and destroying the Samaritan temple. In turn, Samaritans mocked the Jewish holy site in Jerusalem and once actually came into the city by night and defiled it.

In Jesus' day, the feud was as contentious as ever. To Jews, Samaritans represented Israel's downfall. Outside the covenanted mercies of Israel, Samaritans corrupted the Scriptures and worshiped idols on Mount Gerizim. To call one a Samaritan was to call him a heretic, an idolater, and one doomed to hell. Because of this deep-rooted hatred, when Jews wanted to hurl at Jesus the most hateful of insults, they barked, "Aren't we right in saying that you are a Samaritan and demon-possessed?" (John 8:48).

But Jesus saw no reason to live by such cultural prejudices. Samaria was not forbidden territory to Him. He intentionally led His disciples there and sent them on to the nearest town to get their noon meal. Meanwhile He rested at the well—and waited. Wanting to preach good news to the region, He was waiting to meet a Good-News Heart to open the way for Him. He wanted a heart that truly needed hope—and here she came.

Still a long way off, the woman saw someone at the well. *Wouldn't it be my luck. A man is sitting at the well. Maybe he will leave before I get there.* He did not move though. As she drew nearer, she could see that he was a stranger, not even a Samaritan. *Another Jew! What is this? All I need is another self-righteous, contemptuous Jew. What will I do?* One thing she knew: She did not need to experience more cruelty. She would avoid looking at Him, thus denying Him the satisfaction of showing His scorn for her.

Jesus studied the foot-weary, tired-eyed woman as she trudged toward Him. She bore not only the weight of her jug, but also the pain of years of heartache and rejection. Nervously setting her pot on the ground, she took out her leather water container and, stepping forward, began to draw water from the well. She felt the penetrating gaze of this stranger. *Why does He stare at me? What does He want?*

All at once she heard a pleasant voice speak to her. "Will you give me a drink?" he asked politely (John 4:7). This Jew was speaking to *her?* He was asking *her* for a drink? Jewish pride was such that one would endure any hardship rather than ask *anything* of a Samaritan. But Samaritans had pride, too. Her immediate thought may have been something like: *Humph! So a Jew is not above asking help from Samaritans when needing a favor!* However, the kindness in his voice disarmed her. She looked at him and was shocked to meet tender, nonjudgmental eyes.

Jesus had just broken all the rules of Jewish piety. First, women were not highly respected and were often ignored. Jewish men did not speak to women in public. Rarely would a religious teacher even greet his own wife, daughter, or sister on the street. To do so ruined a rabbi's reputation. Asking water of a strange woman who was alone would certainly raise eyebrows. Generally, a man did such a thing only if he hoped or believed she had loose morals.

Second, Samaritans were even more culturally devalued by Jews than women. A devout Jew would never drink from the cup of such a person, considering it contaminated. And even worse, she was a *sinful* Samaritan woman. Despite these facts, it was not beneath Jesus' dignity to reach out to this lonely woman. He would gladly bypass the rules of social and religious propriety to make God's love known to her.

This attitude baffled her. Incredulous, she asked, "You are a Jew and I am a Samaritan woman. How can you ask me for a drink?" (John 4:9).

Rather than answering her question, Jesus left it hanging in the air. Instead, honing in on her true need, He replied, "If you knew the gift of God and who it is that asks you for a drink, you would have asked him and he would have given you living water" (John 4:10).

Gift of God? she may have wondered. *When was the last time anyone, much less God, gave me a gift? Living water? What does he mean?* Everyone knew that "living" water flows from a spring in the earth. She would love to have such a source of pure water. But there were no springs in these parts. The best they had was this well that simply collected ordinary rainwater.

She stared at Jesus. Seeing Him empty-handed, she wondered how He could furnish water of any kind. *What kind of doubletalk is this? First, he asks me for water, and then he claims to have water for me. He doesn't even have a cup!* Seeing His sincerity, however, she knew He wasn't joking.

She thought of the great patriarch Jacob. He had to dig this well one hundred feet deep for water. She frowned, not knowing what to think. "Sir," she said respectfully, "you have nothing to draw with and the well is deep. Where can you get this living water? Are you greater than our father Jacob, who gave us the well and drank from it himself, as did also his sons and his flocks and herds?" (John 4:11-12).

She took Jesus literally, but He spoke spiritually. Seeing her parched heart, He offered her something infinitely more valuable than physical water. He offered her a solution to her deep spiritual needs. He had asked her for help, but His real intent was to help her. He was the well of salvation from which she could draw living water. This "gift" of living water, the Spirit of God, satisfies the thirsty soul. Jesus will give the Holy Spirit freely to those who ask Him.

He understood her spiritual need, but she did not. Responding to her incomprehension, He pointed to Jacob's well and said, "Everyone who drinks this water will be thirsty again, but whoever drinks the water I give him will never thirst. Indeed, the water I give him will become in him a spring of water welling up to eternal life" (John 4:13-14).

Now Jesus had clearly drawn a distinction between the water that temporarily quenches thirsty bodies and that which eternally quenches thirsty souls. This woman and her people had been coming to Jacob's well for physical refreshment for centuries. But they were ignorant of the deeper well of spiritual refreshment. The physical water provided only transient satisfaction. Their thirst soon returned. But Christ's gift of the Spirit is a well of fresh, life-giving water for the soul. If the woman would only drink of this water, her heart's desire would be satisfied by a never-ending fountain of hope and joy, providing her with eternal satisfaction.

She still did not know what Jesus was talking about. But something about Jesus' strange words and manner gripped her. She could feel her heart churn with hope and excitement. *Who is this man? What is this feeling?* While His teaching confused her, it carried with it a force that drove her to desire whatever He offered. Already she was starting to drink into her heart His life-giving words. Already a transforming work had begun. She was filled with longing to know more about this wondrous well He spoke of. He had made her thirsty. "Sir," she said, "give me this water so that I won't get thirsty and have to keep coming here to draw water" (John 4:15).

Jesus let her request dangle for a few moments. He had three objectives for this woman. First, He wanted to make her aware that God had a gift for her; second, He wanted to make her thirsty for that gift; and, third, He wanted to prepare her for receiving the gift. Now that He had completed the first two objectives, He went to the third.

In order for her to receive a revelation of Himself, she first needed a revelation of herself. To see what she could become, she must face who she had been. She had taken water from Jacob's well home with her and bathed in it for as long as she could remember. Yet she was filthy from the stain of sin and needed to wash in the cleansing waters from the well of salvation. Exposing the sinful facts of her life, He sought not to push her to despair, but only to reveal her need. Only then would she be ready for the cure.

Jesus looked at the woman and said, "Go, call your husband and come back" (John 4:16). She had not expected this! Pain cut through her heart. Their conversation had suddenly turned in a direction she did not want to go. As she stood beside Jesus, her sin suddenly appeared so much worse. She could not bring the man she lived with here to see Jesus; nor could she lie to Him. The best she could do was to tell the truth—at least partly.

"I have no husband," she replied. Her answer was evasive, and she hoped He would drop the issue. She nervously bent over the well and began to pull the bucket up.

"You are right when you say you have no husband," Jesus said. "The fact is, you have had five husbands, and the man you now have is not your husband. What you have just said is quite true" (John 4:17-18). Now He had spoken clearly in language she understood!

Stunned, she dropped the rope she was pulling and then glanced up and down the road. Yes, they were still alone. *How did He know that?*

Jesus had unmasked the secret she wanted to keep. Obviously, He had more than a few good reasons to reject this notorious law-breaking Samaritan woman. For she knew the Pentateuch and, therefore, the laws against adultery and immorality. No decent man would have been seen in her company, let alone speak with her.

Her face probably turned red as her humiliating failures were laid out in the open. Christ's ability to see the details of her life staggered her. This meant He could see everything about her—even to the depths of her inmost being. Ashamed, her strength drained out of her. She looked at the ground. *Who IS this man?* Should she wrap the rags of her dignity around her and feign uprightness, or should she let down her defenses and admit the truth?

Jesus had exposed her, but not to mock or condemn. What could describe those penetrating and yet compassionate eyes that she looked into? She felt comfort; she felt hope. "Sir," she said reverently, "I can see that you are a prophet" (John 4:19). Clearly, an inward change was taking place in her heart. She knew there would be no living water for her until she got right with God. *I am a sinner,* she thought. *I need God!* She wanted to be cleansed from her sin, but the only way she knew to find God's forgiveness was through making a sacrifice. But where?

She looked up at Mount Gerizim, a symbol of where God met her people. She had been raised to regard this mountain as the most sacred place on earth and to despise Jerusalem. "Our fathers worshiped on this mountain," she said, "but you Jews claim that the place where we must worship is in Jerusalem" (John 4:20).

Jesus saw that behind her theological observation was a question from her heart: *How can I be made right with God?* He would make no attempt to go back to her moral failures, for He saw her heart's repentance. But she only knew about external religious duties. Where should her sacrifice for sin be made—Mount Gerizim or Jerusalem?

Jesus brought her to see that this question, so important to her, was really now no more than an irrelevant distraction.

Nodding toward the mountain, Jesus declared, "Believe me, woman, a time is coming when you will worship the Father neither on this mountain nor in Jerusalem. You Samaritans worship what you do not know; we worship what we do know, for salvation is from the Jews. Yet a time is coming and has now come when the true worshipers will worship the Father in spirit and truth, for they are the kind of worshipers the Father seeks. God is spirit, and his worshipers must worship in spirit and in truth" (John 4:21-24).

The woman's heart longed for truth, but prophet or not, this talk was too much for her to comprehend. Did He say that nothing could prevent her or anyone else, Jew or Samaritan, from worshiping God directly in spirit and truth? Dizzy with wonder and confusion, she knew that she wanted to be one of these true worshipers. All at once, thoughts of the Messiah came to her mind. The Messiah would make these issues clear. "I know that Messiah . . . is coming," she said. "When he comes, he will explain everything to us" (John 4:25).

Jesus had good news for her! She had not understood it, but only the Messiah could give living water to satisfy the soul's thirst for God. In the messianic age, God's people "will neither hunger nor thirst" (Isa. 49:10). "Water will gush forth in the wilderness and streams in the desert. The burning sand will become a pool, the thirsty ground bubbling springs" (Isa. 35:6-7). Jesus was claiming that He Himself was the Messiah.

But the woman had not yet gotten it. Jesus longed to reveal who He was to her. So He gave no obscure parable. "I who speak to you am he," He declared (John 4:26). He had been teaching and gathering disciples, but it was to this despised Samaritan woman that He unequivocally identified Himself as the Christ, the Anointed One of God.

Her heart nearly stopped. She stood there speechless. Would the Messiah really waste time with a reject from Samaria? It seemed impossible. Yet she believed it was true. Indeed, she had met Truth incarnate, and she had listened to and accepted the truth He gave her. Now the truth would set her free (John 8:32). Jesus had said, "Believe me, woman," and she did. Already He had poured His living water on her parched heart. Drinking in His full revelation, she grabbed hold of the gift only He could give and became a true worshiper of God.

Suddenly a noisy band of men came up the road toward them, the same ones she had seen earlier. The disciples had returned with lunch. When they saw their Lord engaged in a serious conversation with this Samaritan woman, however, they fell silent. They could not believe their eyes. By rabbinic standards, Jesus could not do a more shatteringly unorthodox and disgraceful thing. It was enough that He had sent them into a Samaritan village to buy food—a stretching experience—but now this! He was a great man; that's why they followed Him. Why then would He stoop to speak to *her*? They knew better than to criticize the Lord though, so they said nothing.

The woman was disappointed to have her conversation interrupted by the disciples. She noticed their reaction. She knew what they were thinking. How different the Messiah was from them! But their attitude no longer mattered to her. In Christ she experienced mercy, reconciliation, truth, healing, and freedom from her guilt and shame. It was *all* in Him!

She could barely contain her excitement. Having found this amazing person, she had to share her extraordinary discovery with others. After tasting water from the living well in Christ, she lost her concern for her jar of ordinary water. She set it down. She had a new errand. With the glow of a newborn believer and the passion of an evangelist, she whirled around and flew down the road. She had good news for the town of Sychar!

When she got to town, she was vibrant and filled with fervor. All embarrassment pushed aside, she raced to the public places where she had been ashamed to be seen before and began to call out, "Come,

see a man who told me everything I ever did. Could this be the
Christ?" (John 4:29).

She knew that if she could just get them to come out to the well
and meet Jesus, they would believe. Her personal testimony of His
prophetic gift captured their interest. They might have wondered, *A
prophet told her everything she ever did and still cared about her? This man is
a marvel!* They were more than a little curious, especially when she
asked, "Could this be the Christ?" It was hard enough to think that a
prophet spoke with her, but the great Messiah? How could it be?

Her words were not all that intrigued the townspeople. They
heard good news from her lips, but they also *saw* good news in her face.
They knew her well. They saw the profound change in her, and it was
apparent that she had drunk from some spiritual fountain. She was
happy, bright, effervescent, as if she had met God. They had to see.

Meanwhile Jesus' disciples were concerned for Him: "Rabbi, eat
something." But He replied, "I have food to eat that you know nothing about." Perplexed, they asked each other, "Could someone have
brought him food?" (John 4:31-33).

But Jesus had important spiritual lessons for the men. "My
food," He said, "is to do the will of him who sent me and to finish
his work" (John 4:34). So earnestly did He long for people's souls that
completing His mission to bring them salvation was "food" to Him.
Wanting to impart this same sense of mission to His disciples, He
continued, "Do you not say, 'Four months more and then the harvest'? I tell you, open your eyes and look at the fields! They are ripe
for harvest" (John 4:35).

A multitude of souls sat waiting in the spiritual harvest fields, ripe
for the Gospel. To find them, all the disciples needed to do was lift
up their eyes and look. They had returned from Sychar, bringing no
one with them. But coming up the road they could now plainly see
the woman with The Good-News Heart leading the townspeople of
Sychar to the feet of Jesus.

Many of these Samaritans believed in Christ simply from her testimony, and they urged Him to come stay with them in Sychar. Though Jews never ate or stayed with Samaritans, Jesus went home with them for two days. Hearing His teaching, many more became believers. The living water the woman drank had sprung up into eternal life for her whole community. They told her, "We no longer believe just because of what you said; now we have heard for ourselves, and we know that this man really is the Savior of the world" (John 4:42).

Imagine the love and acceptance these Samaritan people felt from Christ. This is the only time in the Gospels that anyone would confess Jesus Christ as the world's Savior. They had learned firsthand that the good news was for everyone—including them. Now the disciples knew what their Master meant when He spoke of the fields being ripe for harvest.

In the not-too-distant future from this event, Jesus would die on the cross for the sins of the world, including those of the Samaritans. He would rise from the dead and commission His church to proclaim the good news of the Gospel everywhere: "But you will receive power when the Holy Spirit comes on you; and you will be my witnesses in Jerusalem, and in all Judea and Samaria, and to the ends of the earth" (Acts 1:8).

Later when Philip, the evangelist, went to Samaria and preached to crowds, he had amazing success—a Samaritan Pentecost (Acts 8:5-25). Surely he had heard of the Samaritan woman and rejoiced in how God had used her to prepare Samaria's soil for this wondrous time of harvest.

One day on a country road in Samaria, a simple outcast woman with a bruised and battered heart got a private appointment with the Savior of the world. In the biblical record a number of women met their husbands at wells: Rebekah met Isaac, Rachel met Jacob, Zipporah met Moses. But now this Samaritan woman—lost, least, and last—met, not her husband, but the eternal Lover of her soul, Jesus, the Christ. And actually He *was* her Husband to come, inasmuch as she has her place in the Bride of Christ. Running through the village telling everyone about Him, she would become immortalized as the most effective evangelist in the Gospels. Now that's a Good News Heart!

The Spirit of the Sovereign LORD is on me, because the LORD has anointed me to preach good news to the poor.

ISAIAH 61:1

"The time has come," he said. "The kingdom of God is near. Repent and believe the good news!"

MARK 1:15

LESSONS FOR OUR OWN HEARTS

Where were you on September 11, 2001? Like me, you probably will never forget the moment you heard the news. It was about 7:30 A.M. here in the West—just a few days ago as I write this. I had been up late the night before and was still in bed when Clay tore into the room and said, "Your sister just called! Two jets flew into the twin towers of the World Trade Center! The Pentagon has been hit, too! America is under attack!"

I just cried, "What? . . . What? . . . What?" I wanted him to say, "Just kidding," but he did not. I was certain it must be some massive prank on a par with the 1938 "War of the Worlds" radio broadcast that drove millions of panicked Americans to think that hostile Martians had just invaded the land. This, however, was no hoax.

The world rounded the corner into the twenty-first century and a new millennium, and what turbulence and trauma have met us here! In the past several days I have seen our nation's media icons weep. I have heard them say things such as: "This is of an apocalyptic nature," "Our idea of permanence has changed," "The symbol of our economic power has come crashing down." Some might try to think positively, some might fly their flags, some might call in their advice to talk shows, some might sit in strongholds mapping their next great strategy, but what good will any of it do to relieve our national disillusionment, grief, and fear?

The realities of this world have hacked away at our optimism. Those who thought utopia was around the corner, that science would solve every problem have been disillusioned. Those who ascribed to a religion of humanism, with its evolution of human goodness, are left wringing their hands. Things are *not* getting better in this world. How can they when the furious god of this world "knows that his time is short" (see 2 Cor. 4:4; Rev. 12:12 NRSV)? There is just no denying the fact that this is a bad-news world.

Oh, but draw a sigh of relief. We have good news—no, great news! Jesus says, "In this world you will have trouble. But take heart! I have overcome the world" (John 16:33). He reassures us, "When these things begin to take place, stand up and lift up your heads, because your redemption is drawing near" (Luke 21:28). History hastens to its end, yet amid the challenges and uncertainties, we know the Lord of history. Jesus, the true Prophet, Savior, and Lord of all, said that things like this would take place but that we should not get shook up or lose heart. Our hope is infinitely sound and definite, based on His promises, not on what this failing world offers.

Despite the grievous troubles seizing our world (Romans 8:22), we anticipate with joy the birth of God's new order. Very soon heaven's voices will give the triumphant whoop: "The kingdom of this world has become the kingdom of our Lord and of his Christ, and he will reign for ever and ever" (Rev. 11:15). When our mighty Lord and King comes to take us to His glorious eternal home, He will enter our atmosphere in a blaze of glory that lights up the whole universe. This should give us good-news hearts as we face the future!

How can we become good-news people in this bad-news world? Rather than focusing on methods of evangelism—they are important but secondary—let's focus on our hearts. Here are some important considerations.

Hear the Mandate

In my previous book, *Healing for the Heart*, we see how God heals the brokenhearted. Yet, ironically, God wants our hearts to break again, but in a different way. This time He wants our hearts to be broken as His is—for this lost world. People languish in the darkness, lost and dying, while many of us would not think to walk across the street to share the good news with them. In many places, the Gospel is the greatest story *never* told! People might see our Christmas cards but have no idea of the meaning of the words: "I bring you good news of great joy that will be for all the people" (Luke 2:10).

How, then, can they call on the one they have not believed in? And how can they believe in the one of whom they have not heard? And how can they hear without someone preaching to them? And how can they preach unless they are sent? As it is written, "How beautiful are the feet of those who bring good news!"

ROMANS 10:14-15

Jesus said, "Go into all the world and preach the good news to all creation" (Mark 16:15). Who will obey His command in this crucial hour? Who will accept His call to be His ambassadors—to their homes, school campuses, places of work and play, cities, nations— with the light and truth of Jesus Christ? It will take women with good-news hearts. Will you respond to Christ's call? Perhaps you are "ripe," as was the woman at the well, to become a good-news heart whom He can use to reach others.

Drink the Living Water

How do we get from "yearning" to "burning"? We need what the men and women of old possessed—a revelation and impartation of Christ's power, majesty, and incomprehensible love so that our testimony cannot be stopped, no matter what our circumstances. If we do not feel like sharing the good news of the life we have found in

Christ, perhaps our hearts have never truly enjoyed a full revelation of Him. Or perhaps our hearts have grown negligent and become entangled in the things of this world, distracting us from partaking of His living water.

Americans must have watched the jets plow into the World Trade towers hundreds of times in the days following the disaster. Every time we turned on the television, there it was again. This was a tragedy that hit us all deeply, and it was easy to let the reliving of it bury us in despair. As God's people, however, we had to pull ourselves away to meet Jesus at the well of salvation where we could drink in His life, His perspective, His good news. Here the living water could wash over our hearts, revive our spirits, and infuse us with hope.

We cannot be effective in our witness for Christ if we fail to linger with Him at His well of living water where we drink of His Spirit. We desperately need the living water to refresh and enliven our hearts. Without that drink, our words of witness will lack passion and power. Make time to wait on Him. Read God's Word. Spend time in worship and prayer. Open your heart to His presence. "How much more will your Father in heaven give the Holy Spirit to those who ask Him!" (Luke 11:13). This is no luxury; this is your life!

These are the days of Joel, when God is pouring out His Spirit on all flesh, when everyone who calls on His name will be saved (Joel 2:28-29, 32; Acts 2:17-18, 21). Surely we all want to be part of this great move of God's Spirit. The Lord wants a river of living water to bubble out of us to a dry and thirsty land. Refresh yourself in His living water. Drink deeply from the refreshing resource of the Holy Spirit. Cry out, "Come, thou fount of every blessing!"

Look at the Harvest

That day on Samaria's road, Christ said to His disciples, "I tell you, open your eyes and look at the fields! They are ripe for harvest" (John 4:35). Focused on filling their own hungry bellies, the disciples had not yet seen what Christ saw. They saw no ripe fields, especially not in Samaria. Samaria was a bad-news place to them.

Do you see ripe fields? We need to pray for eyes to see and hearts to believe. Sometimes it's easy to think like Elijah in his time of discouragement: "No one is left but me; no one is open to hear the truth" (see 1 Kings 18:22; 19:10, 14, 18). It is true that many people are hardened by sin against the Gospel. Nevertheless, all over the world, including in your neighborhood, there are people ripe to hear about the love of Christ. Every one of us has opportunities to shine our light.

God's Word must be proclaimed in our generation. Recently, as I sat on a bench at my liberal New Age town's plaza, I prayed that God would give me a good-news heart and a good-news opportunity. A young college student who didn't look to me like the type to be open to Christ came near me, and we began to talk. In the course of our conversation, she told me she wanted to come to church and bring her friends. Who was I to think I could draw a profile of those not open to the Gospel? This young woman proved me wrong!

We have a huge challenge ahead of us in our country to seek reconciliation with those who are different from ourselves. God wants to heal the rifts between blacks, whites, Hispanics, Asians, Native Americans, Jews, and other ethnic groups. We have an important role to play as God teaches us not only to tolerate but to love each other. What tests are ahead as we learn to embrace the Arabs among us, too? We need to remember the age-old prayer of St. Francis: "Lord, make me an instrument of your peace. Where there is hatred, let me sow love; where there is injury, pardon. . . ."

Christ has had to deal with the bitter prejudices of His people from the church's inception. Though the Samaritans were foreigners, He loved them and had a good-news heart toward them. He would speak with them, heal them, and even cast them in a positive light in His parable of the Good Samaritan (Luke 10:29-37). He rebuked His disciples for wanting to call down fire from heaven upon the Samaritans (Luke 9:52-55). He deliberately set foot in Samaria and reached out to the woman there, appreciating her unique value. The disciples, however, could not believe that a Samaritan could be saved. Seeing no ripe harvest fields, they likely wanted to hurry through Samaria. They had forgotten how despicable they were themselves, that it was only by grace that Christ had chosen them.

Even after Christ's death, resurrection, and ascension, Peter needed a vision from heaven to convince him to visit Cornelius, an "unclean" Gentile. But God is no respecter of persons, and Peter learned to have a good-news heart toward Gentiles, too. Other apostles called him on the carpet for this. Upon hearing his testimony, they had to acknowledge, "So then, God has granted even the Gentiles repentance unto life" (Acts 11:18). What a revelation! Their eyes *still* had not seen the ripe harvest fields beyond their own prejudices.

"Come, follow me," Jesus said, "and I will make you fishers of men."
MATTHEW 4:19

Do we feel we are too good to share the Gospel with certain elements of society, those outside acceptable circles? Do we dare believe that the good news might reach even the hearts of Muslims, that there is harvesting to be done in their fields, that their souls have great value to God? God loves the Muslims! He remembers them; He sees their pain and needs. Everywhere, regardless of gender, racial, religious, social, or even moral background, He sees precious human beings, very much worth saving and restoring. Jesus told the woman that true worshipers are not marked by such external distinctions but by whether they worship in spirit and in truth.

Today God's Spirit is moving mightily in many parts of the earth to prepare a bride for Christ. In recent decades, multitudes of people have come to Christ. Even so, there are so many places that remain nearly untouched; so much work remains. Yet many in the church are looking toward the heavens, preparing to leave the world; many are looking down, rushing along life's road toward some important destination. But Christ, wanting to win this world, still would direct our gaze outward, saying, "Look at the fields ripe for harvest!"

Hear the Call to Harvest

"God so loved the world," Jesus told Nicodemus. Then He went to the harvest fields of Samaria to prove it. Breaking out of His orthodox Jewish culture, He showed the universality of His Gospel by entering the Samaritan woman's world. Her heart was far from God, and her life was enmeshed in sin, but He had a message of good news for her and all her neighbors. He could have waited for her to seek Him out, but instead He took the initiative. Having come "to seek and to save what was lost" (Luke 19:10), He went out of His way to find her. He waited at the well for her. He opened a conversation with her. Others might have seen her from a worldly perspective—a Samaritan, a woman, a sinner. But Christ saw her through the eyes of infinite love, and to Him she was a precious soul worth dying for. Soon she would be a new creation (see 2 Cor. 5:14-21). He loved the entire town, staying with them until they, too, acknowledged that "this man really is the Savior of the world."

Jesus crossed many barriers to reach these people, and He calls us to cross them, too. He said, "As the Father has sent me, I am sending you" (John 20:21). He sends us to bring good news to the poor, to all those who need God. Do we truly have good-news hearts—hearts that drive us out to the harvest fields? It's one thing to see the harvest fields, another to talk about them, and still another to go to them. The same Christ who invites us, "*Come* to me" (Matt. 11:28), also commands us, "*Go* into all the world" (Mark 16:15) (emphasis mine).

It took awhile for the disciples to hear and understand Christ's call on their lives. He called them to join Him in the harvest fields, and He calls us to do the same. We can get caught up in so many duties in the church, but if we ignore the harvest, we have truly forgotten our primary purpose for existing. Christ has called us. Are you hearing Him?

Know the Urgency of the Hour

This is harvesttime! "Now is the day of salvation" (2 Cor. 6:2). Millions, even billions, of people like the Samaritan woman are waiting at their spiritual wells to meet Jesus. What if He had sat right next to the Samaritan woman and ignored her? Tragically, she would still be hopelessly lost, bound by her sins, with no message of good news to deliver to her people. But that was not the case, thank God! Jesus felt so urgent about the harvest that He ignored His body's need for food and water.

Christ has not changed. He still longs to reach people all over the world who are longing for hope, needing us to tell them the good news. He calls us to reach out to them, letting them know that He is alive, waiting at the well of salvation to give them life.

The woman at the well picked up on His urgency. Leaving her water jar behind, she rushed headlong to the harvest field. So urgent was the Early Church about the harvest fields that they "turned the world upside down" for Christ (Acts 17:6 NRSV). Everywhere they went, they shared the Gospel.

There is an urgency in times of harvest because no one knows how long they will last. What is ripe soon rots or is devoured by pests. And once the harvest is lost, it cannot be recovered. So the work must be done right away. Similarly, the hour is late for our world's harvest. Our harvesttime is drawing to a close. If souls under conviction are not met with God's truth and love, they will perish, many being devoured by false religions. How many have perished already because Christ's laborers never picked up the sense of urgency?

We are coming to that time when people will no longer listen to the truth. Can you hear the urgency in Paul's words to Timothy? "I solemnly urge you: proclaim the message; be persistent whether the time is favorable or unfavorable. . . . For the time is coming when people will not put up with sound doctrine . . . and will turn away from listening to the truth and wander away to myths. As for you . . . do the work of an evangelist" (2 Tim. 4:1-5 NRSV).

What about us? The brevity of the time left for harvesting should give us utmost urgency about our task. Do you have other things to do? So did Christ; so did the woman of Samaria. Let the harvest interrupt you. Make it your priority. Today is the day of salvation! Today is the year of the favor of our God! To let this urgent hour pass us by without giving it our best is inexcusable.

Overcome the Hindrances

Many believers are complacent and won't bother with the harvest. Others, however, genuinely want good-news hearts and yet are hindered in some way from entering the harvest. Of all such hindrances, fear has got to be the greatest. We fear personal rejection; we fear we won't know the answers to people's questions or challenges; we fear we won't come across in the right way—we fear! We must stop letting our fears of how we will appear to unbelievers or how they will respond to us dictate our response to the harvest.

I will never forget a disappointing lesson the Lord taught me one day. As I sat in my Jewish doctor's waiting room, the Holy Spirit impressed on me that I should share my faith with him. But he seemed smug and arrogant to me, and I had never liked him. The biggest problem, however, was that I could not imagine subjecting myself to the humiliating rejection I expected from him. *This could not be God. Dr. L is Jewish, extremely rich, handsome, and cocky. He would never be open.* To my relief, the impression passed (God never coerces us).

A year later I had to see the doctor again. I had come this time because I had done something stupid and was suffering for it. As I sheepishly shared my experience with him, expecting him to bark at me, he surprised me. Instead, I detected warmth in him I had never before seen. Far from belittling or reprimanding me, he gently encouraged me. Finally I could stand it no longer. "You seem different to me," I said. Without hesitation he replied, "I accepted Jesus Christ as my Savior, and He's changed my life." I asked how this had happened, and he said that about a year earlier his sister-in-law had shared the Gospel with him. I felt as if the Lord had just walloped me with a two-by-four. He had invited me to participate in this miracle, and I had refused. What a blessing I had missed!

We can invent so many plausible-sounding excuses to justify our fear: "I need to wait till he is ready." "This is not the right time. I don't want to turn her off." "God's Word says not to cast pearls before swine." "That's not my gift." How my excuse fell to the ground. The truth was, I simply did not have enough love in my heart for Jesus or for a lost Jewish doctor. The only force greater than fear—love— would have conquered my fear. Love humbles us, heals us, and propels us to share our faith.

Love will overcome every hindrance. It will motivate us to join Christ in His labor of love for souls. If we have not love, we are nothing and have nothing to offer (see 1 Cor. 13). Jesus warned that in the end times, "the love of most will grow cold" (Matt. 24:12). We must keep the flame of love burning in our hearts.

Get to Work in the Harvest

In the story of the woman at the well, we can see two methods of outreach: one-on-one and mass evangelism! Both worked. Jesus reached the woman, and she was His ambassador in reaching her whole community. What we do not see here is people doing nothing.

Whoever turns a sinner from the error of his way will save him from death and cover over a multitude of sins.

JAMES 5:20

The woman did not wait till she felt more whole or got more training. Seeing her opportunity, she seized it. It meant extra effort for

her, but she could not just let Christ go away. Her neighbors *had* to
meet Him!

Though we should seek training and a good theological ground-
ing, a lack of these does not exempt us from sharing Christ now. Just
look at the woman! She was an outcast, a byword, fodder for gossip,
the biggest nobody in town. But she had a good-news heart. Her
great desire to tell others overran her sense of unworthiness. She
didn't understand it all; she didn't have all her facts straight. But she
knew enough—enough not to hold the good news to herself, enough
to share Christ with others. Hearing her testimony and seeing the
change in her, the people went to investigate Christ's claims for
themselves.

Are *you* sharing Christ with others? If not, what is *your* excuse? If
you have received good news, then spread good news. If Christ has
shared His life with you, then you can do Him the honor of sharing
Him with others. Don't feel unworthy or inadequate to work in His
harvest. Just share what He means to you, like the woman did. Even
with a fledgling faith, God can use you. All you need to do is open
your mouth and point the way to Jesus. With your good-news heart,
you can make people thirsty. You can make them aware that they need
Christ. Let people see the change in you, and use the opportunity to
introduce them to Christ. Even a little spark can set a forest ablaze.

Tell them, "Jesus Christ has changed my life, and He wants to
change yours, too. Come and see!" Often it's as simple as that!

One More Word About Living Water

Christ says, "Freely you have received, freely give" (Matt. 10:8). He
gives to us; we give to others. He also said, "Give, and it will be given
to you" (Luke 6:38). We give to others; Christ gives to us. Can you
see the cycle of blessing? Sharing the good news is part of the natural flow of God's blessings in His kingdom. It is in our giving that we
find our supplies replenished. As we overcome our inhibitions, stepping out to labor in the harvest, a great deal comes back to us! Our

tired, sagging faith quickly enlivens. We felt dried out, burned out, fizzled out, but suddenly we feel revived. Clearly, sharing Christ with others is good for our own souls, infusing us with renewed life.

My family used to live near a river, and we had a great little swimming hole for a while. It was deep enough for jumping off the rocks with our dog into the sparkling water, and we simply loved it. One year, however, a gravel company did some digging and changed the course of the river. We returned to our swimming hole the next summer and were horrified at what we found. It was still there, but the water was stagnant! Without adequate water flowing in or out, it had turned slimy green and dreadful. Unable to see the bottom, I was afraid of what might be down there—dead animal carcasses, for all I knew. There was no way in the world you could get me into that murky water!

Think of the spiritual realm. Wanting the springs of living water, some cry, "Give me more, Lord!" But the Holy Spirit refuses to pour Himself into a place that is bottled up with no outflow. Standing water soon stagnates. Obviously, He will not fill a place that moss and little critters will soon overtake, where the water will turn gross, undrinkable, even stinking. He *hates* stagnation!

Jesus said, "But you will receive power when the Holy Spirit comes on you; and you will be my witnesses" (Acts 1:8). See the outflow? By nature, living water must empty into the world. It was never intended for the church's sole enjoyment. Christianity is not a stagnant, dead religion. It is not even ordinary faith supplied by water sitting in the bottom of an old well. Living water is free-flowing, refreshing, alive; everywhere it touches it brings life. What blessing we enjoy as this precious living water flows into us and through us.

Don't worry about the results of your witnessing. Leave those to God. You keep the living water flowing. As you keep sharing the good news, you will ensure that the truth will never stagnate in your heart. You will experience a wellspring of living water bubbling up into an overflowing, ever-flowing fountain in your heart.

> Water will gush forth in the wilderness and streams in the desert. The
> burning sand will become a pool, the thirsty ground bubbling springs.
>
> ISAIAH 35:6-7

A Soul's Worth

Think of all the "important" appointments that got canceled on
September 11, 2001. Suddenly none of them mattered anymore. Our
entire nation sat watching and praying as networks broadcast the riv-
eting images of thousands of rescue workers and volunteers at
"ground zero" poring through the tons of rubble that had been our
World Trade towers. In the early hours five people were rescued, and
who could measure the joy and celebration that erupted over these!

Spurred on by these few successes, rescuers labored frantically,
hour after hour, day in and day out, afraid to quit. Perhaps beneath
the next steel beam was someone still waiting to be rescued. They had
to find that person! Exhausted, they kept working, hoping against
hope to pull out a miracle. They would have paid any price for it. In
fact, they did. Worming their way through tiny passages beneath the
rubble, they risked their very lives every minute. But that did not stop
them. How they wanted to hand their mayor some good news. But
each day hopes dimmed, and the mayor grew graver and graver.
Finally everyone knew the window of opportunity had passed. It was
simply too late for that one last rescue.

What is one soul worth to you? Jesus took time one day at Jacob's
well to reach one immortal soul. He died for that soul's salvation.
Now He looks to us to do our part. In the spiritual realm, there is a
crisis of cosmic proportions. Billions of souls stand in the balance.
Christ's loving heart breaks for them. He wants to broadcast joyfully
to the heavens that these lost souls are being rescued from eternal
death. The days are slipping by. He urges us on, saying, "As long as it
is day, we must do the work of him who sent me. Night is coming,
when no one can work" (John 9:4).

Until that curtain of night drops, we must work diligently. Yet ours is not a fruitless, depressing search. This is still harvesttime when fields are ripe for picking. All heaven stands on tiptoe, watching our progress. Jesus gives us a small glimpse: "I tell you, there is rejoicing in the presence of the angels of God over one sinner who repents" (Luke 15:10).

Will you give the angels something to rejoice over? Will you let Christ fill you with a good-news heart? Will you look around and see the fields ripe for harvesting? Will you do your part to spread the good news to the ends of the earth? Will you pray, "Holy Spirit, I want more of You in my life. I want more of You to flow into me so more of You will flow out through me to this lost and dying world"?

A society largely at war with God, America has suffered deep wounds. She needs to hear of sin and salvation. She needs the ministry of "salty" Christians (see Matt. 5:13; Mark 9:50) who are winsome and flavorful, who do not rub their salt in her wounds. Nor does she need us to offer false hope. I have heard Christians express the idea that everyone who died in the towers that day went to heaven. Would that this were so! People who say that need to read John 3:16 again. If everyone were saved, then our task would not be urgent. The fact is, people from many nations, including our own, perished that day without Christ. Let this be a wake-up call to the church. With good-news hearts, let's reach our generation for Christ.

The fruit of the righteous is a tree of life, and he who wins souls is wise.

PROVERBS 11:30

Jesus promises many rewards for entering His harvest force. He says, "Even now the reaper draws his wages" (John 4:36). These wages are beyond describing. The joy of bringing souls to Christ is blessing enough, but God also enriches our lives in many other ways. Not only that, one day soon we will enter into the joy of the Lord with souls in our account. What a joyful time that will be!

Just as the woman ran home to preach the good news, so it has been with countless others since then. Whether in time of war or peace, famine or plenty, distress or calm, touched by the love of Jesus Christ, they have published the Gospel throughout the world. Now the baton has passed to us. Ours is a precious privilege but also a grave responsibility. This is a frightening, critical hour for our nation and world. But the rock-solid truth of Christ still shines brightly. Whether the best of times or the worst, God needs us to spread this good news. Before the end comes, Jesus wants everyone in this world to hear His offer of eternal life.

The Spirit and the bride say, "Come!" And let him who hears say, "Come!" Whoever is thirsty, let him come; and whoever wishes, let him take the free gift of the water of life.

REVELATION 22:17

And this gospel of the kingdom will be preached in the whole world as a testimony to all nations, and then the end will come.

MATTHEW 24:14

Heart Check

1. Do you consider yourself as having a good-news heart? Do you think unbelievers you know would agree?

2. How can you better tap into God's provision of living water?

3. Have you decided to join Christ in His harvest? What harvest field has He shown you?

4. Has anything kept you from the harvest in the past? Describe how you can now work to overcome hindrances.

5. With whom can you share the good news today?

6. Compose a prayer to God in response to this chapter's lessons.

NOTES

2 THE SYROPHOENICIAN WOMAN

1. Karen Loritts, "A Legacy of Tenacity," in Barbara Rainey and Ashley Escue, *A Mother's Legacy* (Nashville: Thomas Nelson, 2000), pp. 35, 36.

5 QUEEN ESTHER

1. The Greek historian Herodotus notes that Xerxes' father, Darius, received nearly fifteen thousand talents of silver in revenue in an entire year. Haman could not have owned this much money himself. He probably intended to get it by seizing and selling off the property of the slain Jews.

6 PRISCILLA

1. Robert Young, *Young's Literal Translation of the Bible* (Grand Rapids, Mich.: Baker/Revell, 1989).

2. Greek interlinear version used in *The Zondervan Parallel New Testament in Greek and English,* trans. and ed. Alfred Marshall (Grand Rapids, Mich.: Zondervan, 1980), 481, 631.

3. *Ante-Nicene Fathers,* vol. 4, book 1, chapter 1, "Introduction. Modesty in Apparel Becoming to Women, in Memory of the Introduction of Sin into the World Through a Woman." www.ccel.org

4. Charles Colson, "Why Women Like Big Government," *Christianity Today*, November 11, 1996.

5. Leslie K. Tarr, "Models of Compassion and Courage," Women in Church History series, *Decision*, December 1994.

7 THE WOMAN WITH TWO MITES

1. "Hark, the Voice of Jesus Calling" by Daniel March; "How Shall I Sing That Majesty?" by John Mason; "Take My Life, and Let It Be" by Frances R. Havergal. All are in public domain.

2. Barna Research Group, "Churches Lose Financial Ground in 2000," June 2001. Used by permission.

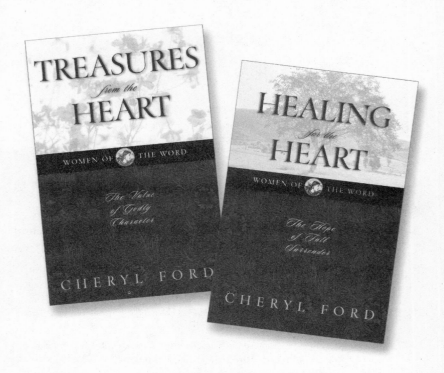

Women of the Word

Our walk with God begins in the quiet reaches of our hearts. It is there that He whispers His love for us. His desires for us. His treasures and His purpose and His healing. Cheryl Ford takes you through the stories of several biblical women and shows how their hearts responded to God's voice in their lives. As you get to know your sisters of faith better, you will come to discover the same truth they did: that when you fully open your heart to God, He fills it abundantly with Himself.

Treasures from the Heart
Healing for the Heart
Triumphs of the Heart